Biography Today

*Profiles
of People
of Interest
to Young
Readers*

Volume 12
Issue 2
April 2003

Cherie D. Abbey
Managing Editor

Omnigraphics

*615 Griswold Street
Detroit, Michigan 48226*

Cherie D. Abbey, *Managing Editor*

Sheila Fitzgerald, Leif Gruenberg, Laurie Lanzen Harris,
Kevin Hile, Kevin Hillstrom, Laurie Hillstrom, Sarah Lorenz,
and Sue Ellen Thompson *Staff Writers*

Barry Puckett, *Research Associate*

Allison A. Beckett and Linda Strand, *Research Assistants*

Omnigraphics, Inc.

* * *

Matthew P. Barbour, *Senior Vice President*
Kay Gill, *Vice President — Directories*
Kevin Hayes, *Operations Manager*
Leif Gruenberg, *Development Manager*
David P. Bianco, *Marketing Consultant*

* * *

Peter E. Ruffner, *Publisher*
Frederick G. Ruffner, Jr., *Chairman*

Copyright © 2003 Omnigraphics, Inc.
ISSN 1058-2347

The information in this publication was compiled from the sources cited and from other sources considered reliable. While every possible effort has been made to ensure reliability, the publisher will not assume liability for damages caused by inaccuracies in the data, and makes no warranty, express or implied, on the accuracy of the information contained herein.

This book is printed on acid-free paper meeting the ANSI Z39.48 Standard. The infinity symbol that appears above indicates that the paper in this book meets that standard.

Printed in the United States

INDEXED IN
Children's Magazine Guide

Contents

Preface

Biography Today is a magazine designed and written for the young reader—ages 9 and above—and covers individuals that librarians and teachers tell us that young people want to know about most: entertainers, athletes, writers, illustrators, cartoonists, and political leaders.

The Plan of the Work

The publication was especially created to appeal to young readers in a format they can enjoy reading and readily understand. Each issue contains approximately 10 sketches arranged alphabetically. Each entry provides at least one picture of the individual profiled, and bold-faced rubrics lead the reader to information on birth, youth, early memories, education, first jobs, marriage and family, career highlights, memorable experiences, hobbies, and honors and awards. Each of the entries ends with a list of easily accessible sources designed to lead the student to further reading on the individual and a current address. Obituary entries are also included, written to provide a perspective on the individual's entire career. Obituaries are clearly marked in both the table of contents and at the beginning of the entry.

Biographies are prepared by Omnigraphics editors after extensive research, utilizing the most current materials available. Those sources that are generally available to students appear in the list of further reading at the end of the sketch.

Indexes

A new index now appears in all *Biography Today* publications. In an effort to make the index easier to use, we have combined the **Name** and **General Index** into one, called the **Cumulative Index**. This new index contains the names of all individuals who have appeared in *Biography Today* since the series began. The names appear in bold faced type, followed by the issue in which they appeared. The General Index also contains the occupations, nationalities, and ethnic and minority origins of individuals profiled. The General Index is cumulative, including references to all individuals who have appeared in the *Biography Today* General Series and the *Biography Today* Special Subject volumes since the series began in 1992.

In a further effort to consolidate and save space, the Birthday and Places of Birth Indexes will be appearing only in the September issue and in the Annual Cumulation.

Our Advisors

This series was reviewed by an Advisory Board comprised of librarians, children's literature specialists, and reading instructors to ensure that the concept of this publication—to provide a readable and accessible biographical magazine for young readers—was on target. They evaluated the title as it developed, and their suggestions have proved invaluable. Any errors, however, are ours alone. We'd like to list the Advisory Board members, and to thank them for their efforts.

Sandra Arden, *Retired*
Assistant Director
Troy Public Library, Troy, MI

Gail Beaver
University of Michigan School of Information
Ann Arbor, MI

Marilyn Bethel, *Retired*
Broward County Public Library System
Fort Lauderdale, FL

Nancy Bryant
Brookside School Library,
Cranbrook Educational Community
Bloomfield Hills, MI

Cindy Cares
Southfield Public Library
Southfield, MI

Linda Carpino
Detroit Public Library
Detroit, MI

Carol Doll
Wayne State University Library and Information Science Program
Detroit, MI

Helen Gregory
Grosse Pointe Public Library
Grosse Pointe, MI

Jane Klasing, *Retired*
School Board of Broward County
Fort Lauderdale, FL

Marlene Lee
Broward County Public Library System
Fort Lauderdale, FL

Sylvia Mavrogenes
Miami-Dade Public Library System
Miami, FL

Carole J. McCollough
Detroit, MI

Rosemary Orlando
St. Clair Shores Public Library
St. Clair Shores, MI

Renee Schwartz
Broward County Public Library System
Fort Lauderdale, FL

Lee Sprince
Broward West Regional Library
Fort Lauderdale, FL

Susan Stewart, *Retired*
Birney Middle School Reading Laboratory, Southfield, MI

Ethel Stoloff, *Retired*
Birney Middle School Library
Southfield, MI

Our Advisory Board stressed to us that we should not shy away from controversial or unconventional people in our profiles, and we have tried to follow their advice. The Advisory Board also mentioned that the sketches might be useful in reluctant reader and adult literacy programs, and we would value any comments librarians might have about the suitability of our magazine for those purposes.

Your Comments Are Welcome

Our goal is to be accurate and up-to-date, to give young readers information they can learn from and enjoy. Now we want to know what you think. Take a look at this issue of *Biography Today,* on approval. Write or call me with your comments. We want to provide an excellent source of biographical information for young people. Let us know how you think we're doing.

Cherie Abbey
Managing Editor, *Biography Today*
Omnigraphics, Inc.
615 Griswold Street
Detroit, MI 48226

editor@biographytoday.com
www.biographytoday.com

Congratulations!

Congratulations to the following individuals and libraries, who are receiving a free copy of *Biography Today*, Vol. 12, No. 2 for suggesting people who appear in this issue:

Carol Arnold, Hoopeston Public Library, Hoopeston, IL
Vondell Ashton, Washington, DC
Karina Avina, Northhighlands, CA
S. Backus, Brooklyn, NY
Ayanna Black, Southfield, MI
Susan Caldwell, Evansville, IN
Lauren Darrow, Alpharetta, GA
Bridget E. Doughtery, Wyomissing, PA
Nichole Eason, Laconia, IN
Ashlee Glastetter, Chaffee, MO
Marti Ingvarsson, Grayling, MI
Leigh Jordan, Lancaster, SC
Johnny Missakian, Fresno, CA
Janice P. Saulsby, Dr. Phillips High School, Orlando, FL
Janet A. Speziale, Hilltop Elementary School Library, Lodi, NJ
Autumn Tompkins, Allegan, MI
Miranda Trimm, Allegan, MI
Rose Walker, Brownsburg, IN

Yolanda Adams 1961-

American Gospel Singer
Creator of the Award-Winning Albums *Mountain
High . . . Valley Low*, *The Experience*, and *Believe*

BIRTH

Yolanda Adams was born on August 27, 1961, in Houston,
Texas. Her mother, Carolyn Adams, was a schoolteacher who
gave piano lessons on the side and was the gospel pianist for
their local church. Her father, Major Adams, was also a teacher

who coached sports at a middle school. Yolanda was the oldest of the Adamses' six children. She has three younger brothers and two younger sisters.

YOUTH

Life in the Adams family revolved around religion and music. Yolanda's mother had been a music major in college, and she exposed her children to all kinds of music. They listened to "everything from Stevie Wonder to Beethoven," Yolanda says — including classical symphonies, rhythm-and-blues, jazz, and modern gospel. At age three, Yolanda sang her first solo, "Jesus Loves the Little Children," in the Baptist church where her mother played the piano and her father sang in the choir. "Our family was always in church," Yolanda recalls. Their involvement in church activities kept the Adams children close to their parents and away from what she calls "the negative elements" in Houston society.

> ― " ―
>
> *After her father's death, Yolanda joined a youth gospel group. "My brother's godmother knew how close [my dad and I] were, and she thought it would be a good outlet for me, so she convinced my mom to let me try out for the choir, and I made the audition." Although she had lots of experience performing with her church's choir, Yolanda says she started out "singing with my head down, looking at my shoes, just all nervous."*
>
> ― " ―

When Yolanda was just a young teenager, her father, Major Adams, taught her how to write checks, pay bills, and invest her money, just in case anything ever happened to him. Four months later, he died from complications following a car accident. Yolanda was only 13 at the time. Her mother was so overwhelmed by grief that Yolanda had to make all the funeral arrangements and take care of her five younger siblings. She says that without her faith in God, she never could have gotten through this difficult period in her life.

Not long after her father's death, Yolanda joined the Southeast Inspirational Choir, a youth gospel group made up of young singers from Houston-area churches. "My brother's godmother knew how close [my dad and I] were, and she thought it would be a good outlet for me," Yolanda explains, "so she convinced my mom to let me try out for the choir, and I made the audition." Although she had lots of experience performing with her church's

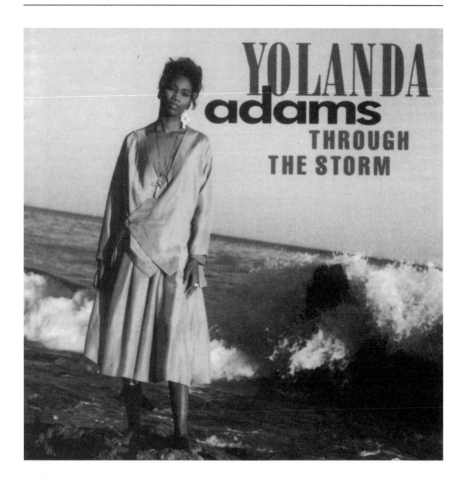

choir, Yolanda says she started out "singing with my head down, looking at my shoes, just all nervous." Despite her shyness, she soon became a lead singer for the Choir. In 1980 their first big hit, "My Liberty," featured a solo by Adams.

EDUCATION

As a student at Sterling High School in Houston, Yolanda dreamed of be-coming a model. With her good looks and height of more than six feet, that dream seemed well within her reach. But her grandfather told her that as the oldest of her family's six children, she should set a good example for her siblings by going to college. So after graduating from high school in 1979, she went to her father's alma mater, Texas Southern University. She majored in radio and television communications there, planning to be-

11

come a television news anchor. After serving as an intern at a local television station during her senior year, she was confident of getting a full-time job there when she graduated. But the job fell through, so she decided to follow in her parents' footsteps and become a teacher. She went back to school and got her teaching certificate. She graduated from Texas Southern University in 1983.

Some years later, in 1997, Adams enrolled in Howard University's divinity program to earn her master's degree. But by then her singing career was taking up so much of her time that she had to discontinue her studies.

"I got a chance to see kids on all levels: suburbanite, upper middle class, [and] poor, inner-city kids," Adams says about her years teaching elementary school. "I was teaching school during the week and singing on the weekends. So I had the best of everything."

BECOMING A GOSPEL SINGER

After graduating from Texas Southern, Adams taught second and third grade at Patterson Elementary School for seven years. "I got a chance to see kids on all levels: suburbanite, upper middle class, [and] poor, inner-city kids," she recalls. At the same time, she continued to sing with the Southeast Inspirational Choir. "I was teaching school during the week and singing on the weekends," she says. "So I had the best of everything."

In 1986 Thomas Whitfield, a well-known gospel producer and composer, heard Adams sing with the Choir and offered to help her produce an album. The result was *Just As I Am,* released by Sound of Gospel Records the following year. The album stayed on the Billboard gospel chart for two years and was in the Top Ten for eight months. This caught the attention of Tribute Records, a gospel label that signed Adams to a five-record deal. They produced her second album, *Through the Storm,* in 1991. Adams had written or co-written most of the songs on this album, which won two Dove Awards from the Gospel Music Association and was nominated for a Grammy Award.

By 1992 Adams was earning more from her singing career than from her teaching job, so she decided to leave her job and focus on singing. "It took all the courage I had," she says of her decision. "I never dreamed of leaving the school system, and when I did it was a huge step, but I'm so glad I took that step on faith."

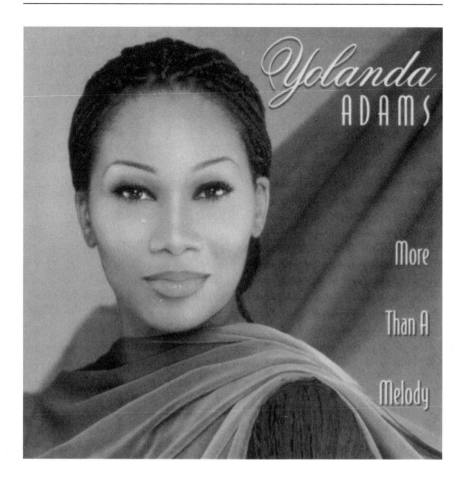

CAREER HIGHLIGHTS

Since that time, Adams has built a successful career as a top gospel singer. Her next release, *Save the World* (1993), showcased her powerful voice and unique way of combining traditional gospel music with contemporary pop and salsa rhythms. She wrote or collaborated on most of its songs, which dealt not only with faith and spirituality but with the problems that confront Christians in today's world. One of the songs, for example, was inspired by a teenage girl in Adams's church who committed suicide, while others dealt with loneliness and depression. Rather than limiting herself to the subject matter of traditional gospel music, she pointed out, "I like to deal with issues that people are facing." *Save the World* was even more successful than her earlier releases, winning three Stellar Gospel Music Awards. It became a top-selling album, spending more than a year on Billboard's gospel chart.

More Than a Melody

Although she had already made three albums, it wasn't until *More Than a Melody* was released in 1995 that people began to think of Adams as more than a gospel singer. This album showed the influence of such pop singers as Anita Baker and Whitney Houston. It also included a re-make of the 1970 Steve Miller hit "Fly Like an Eagle," as well as the rap-inspired "Gotta Have Love." The basic message was still a Christian one. But it was also clear that Adams was trying to reach a broader audience by interspersing jazz and R&B songs with more traditional gospel tunes. When accused of making a "secular" (non-religious) album, Adams replied, "In order to get kids listening to gospel you've got to give them what they're used to listening to." Kids want to hear music with rhythms they recognize, she explained, "so I have to have something in there with a beat."

> —— *"* ——
>
> *"In ordered to get kids listening to gospel you've got to give them what they're used to listening to," Adams says. Kids want to hear music with rhythms they recognize, "so I have to have something in there with a beat."*
>
> —— *"* ——

More Than a Melody sold more that 100,000 copies and marked a turning point in Adams's career. It led to invitations to perform on the 1996 Soul Train Music Awards, the 1997 Essence Awards, and *The Tonight Show.* President Bill Clinton invited her to sing at a White House Christmas celebration, where she was given a standing ovation, and contemporary gospel singer Kirk Franklin invited her to join his "Tour of Life" stage review. Franklin had made history in 1993 when he became the first singer since Aretha Franklin to sell a million copies of a gospel album. Touring with Kirk Franklin gave Adams a chance to observe an artist who had "crossed over" to a more contemporary, mainstream style without abandoning his roots in traditional gospel music.

In 1996 Adams made what was supposed to be a concert video in front of a live congregation at a church in Washington, D.C. People who had heard her sing began calling the recording company to say that they wanted to listen to her music in their cars, and it soon became clear that she had another album in the works. *Yolanda . . . Live in Washington* sold more than 150,000 copies and brought Adams a second Grammy nomination and a Stellar Award. It was followed two years later by *Songs From the Heart,* a collection of standard gospel songs and hymns interpreted in Adams's own unique

way. This was the last of the five albums she was under contract to record with Tribute/Diadem Records, so Adams began looking around for a recording company that would bring her music to a wider audience.

Joining the Mainstream

One such company was Elektra Records, which had produced albums for such well-known artists as Tracy Chapman, Natalie Cole, and Missy Elliott. Sylvia Rhone, an executive for Elektra, had heard Adams perform with the "Tour of Life" in New York. When Rhone signed her to a five-record contract, Adams became the label's first gospel artist. Rhone compared her to such legendary female vocalists as Dinah Washington, Nancy Wilson, Sarah Vaughan, and Whitney Houston, predicting that Yolanda Adams would be just as famous some day. Elektra was definitely a "mainstream"

Adams performs at the Soul Train Music Awards, March 2002.

label. But unlike other recording companies that had approached Adams in the past, Elektra was not interested in forcing her to change her style or her message to increase her appeal to secular audiences.

Mountain High . . . Valley Low, Adams's first album with Elektra, was released in 1999. It gave her an opportunity to team up with top R&B and pop producers like Keith Thomas, who had worked with Vanessa Williams and Wynonna Judd, and Jimmy Jam & Terry Lewis, who had produced Janet Jackson and Mary J. Blige. With Jam and Lewis she sang the contemporary soul ballad "Open My Heart," in which she asks God for spiritual guidance. The song was picked up by a number of pop and R&B radio stations and became her first big crossover hit, winning a Soul Train Lady of Soul Award for Best R&B/Soul Song. "What surprised me was how many people needed to hear that song," Adams told *Essence* magazine. "It spoke to so many people, so many ages, so many hearts." Also on the album were hip-hop-influenced songs like "Time to Change" and "Yeah," along with others in which jazz and R&B elements could clearly be heard.

Mountain High . . . Valley Low became Adams's "coming out" album, selling more than a million copies and winning a Grammy Award. It was praised for being "both uplifting and inspirational," and it helped disprove the myth that women gospel singers couldn't sell as many albums as men. "Few vocalists can match the range, power, and control of this 38-year-old singer, and these new pop-funk beats give that voice the showcase it deserves," observed the reviewer for the *Washington Post*. The wide exposure the album received on television and mainstream radio stations reassured Adams that she had made the right decision in signing with Elektra. "I need to be in a place where my message can be heard by everyone," she said. At the same time, she made it clear that she had no intention of becoming another Whitney Houston. "As a Christian," she explained, "I'm not supposed to be like everybody else or follow what's going on. I am supposed to tread new ground. I'm out to give God his just due, and my goal is to show people how really cool God is."

Recent Releases

Adams released *Christmas with Yolanda Adams* in 2000, a compilation that featured both gospel hymns and traditional Christmas songs, often with a contemporary R&B sound. After that, she made another live recording in 2001. She had been traveling with the first all-female gospel tour, "Sisters in the Spirit," and her performance at Constitution Hall in Washington D.C

—— " ——

"What surprised me was how many people needed to hear that song," Adams said about her ballad *"Open My Heart,"* in which she asks God for spiritual guidance. *"It spoke to so many people, so many ages, so many hearts."*

—— " ——

became her next live album, *The Experience*. Although Adams was criticized for releasing another album so soon after *Mountain High . . . Valley Low*—especially one that contained seven of the same songs—it won a Grammy Award for Best Contemporary Soul Gospel Album.

Later that same year, Adams released her tenth album, *Believe*. This, too, included some of the same songs that were originally heard on *Mountain High . . . Valley Low*, but it also featured R&B-flavored pop, ballads, and gospel tunes with a gospel choir singing backup. Adams co-wrote four of the songs, including one called "Darling Girl," written as a tribute to motherhood and the birth of her first child. The album as a whole received mixed reviews, but it still debuted at No. 1 on the Billboard gospel charts and won the Soul Train "Lady of Soul" Award for Best Gospel Album.

Reaching Out to Young People

Like the schoolteacher she used to be, Adams has put just as much energy into helping young people as she has into her music career. She is very involved with the FILA athletic wear company's youth outreach program, Operation Rebound. With this program, she visits inner-city schools and speaks to the students about the dangers of substance abuse and the importance of staying in school and getting an education.

Adams has also formed her own management company, Mahogany Entertainment, to help young people who are just starting out as gospel performers. "Our goal is to bring mentorship to young people in gospel music," she explains. She tries to bring their talents to the attention of record companies so that they are well represented and don't have to struggle as hard to get noticed or worry about being taken advantage of.

Some day Adams would like to open an all-girls Christian school with an emphasis on the performing arts. She would also like to build a children's art center in Houston. "I'm hoping my success in the music field can make that happen," she says.

Devoted to Gospel

Despite frequent complaints from fans who accuse her of abandoning gospel for pop, Adams remains devoted to gospel music. She says she will remain true to it for two reasons: "The first reason is that I've never had a desire to sing anything other than gospel music. The second is that I believe we can make gospel just as popular as country music is now." To achieve this, she knows that she will have to show that there is more to gospel music than "choir robes and folks shouting."

"You can't sell beyond the gospel community without alienating that gospel audience," Adams admits. "You just have to have the right song. For artists who are involved in gospel, the whole point is to encourage people to make their lives better, to lift them up. How better to do that than to sing to someone?" She believes that since the terrorist attacks of September 11, 2001, more people have turned to gospel music for comfort and inspiration, and that its popularity will continue to grow during these troubled times.

> *"For artists who are involved in gospel, the whole point is to encourage people to make their lives better, to lift them up. How better to do that than to sing to someone?"*

MARRIAGE AND FAMILY

Adams was first married in 1988. But she felt that she was making a mistake almost from the start, and they divorced after only two years. In 1997 she married former New York Jets football player Tim Crawford, Jr., whom she had known since she was 16. They never really lost touch, and when both of them ended up divorced in their 30s, their relationship changed from friendship to romance. Crawford, who now works as a financial advisor, has a teenage daughter from a previous marriage named Ashley, and in January 2001 he and Yolanda had their first child, a girl named Taylor Ayanna. They still live in the Houston area, within a 20-mile radius of Yolanda's mother and five siblings.

Adams at the Soul Train Awards with her daughter Taylor, February 2001.

MAJOR INFLUENCES

Adams says that one of her greatest influences was Rosa Parks, the now-famous African-American civil rights heroine. Adams was only seven years old when Parks refused to give up her seat to a white passenger and move to the back of a public bus in Montgomery, Alabama. Her action helped to spark the civil rights movement. "I think Rosa touched my life in a very strong way," she says, "because I knew that I didn't have to bend or bow down. . . . I could be a strong person, especially a strong black woman."

As far as her music is concerned, Adams says that she has been influenced by a wide range of singers. "I take my jazz from Nancy Wilson, my gospel and R&B from people like Aretha [Franklin], my pop from Celine Dion, and my country from Reba McEntire." Her favorite singers also include Stevie Wonder and Donny Hathaway.

FAVORITE ALBUMS

Adams's favorite album is gospel singer Tramaine Hawkins's *Highway to Heaven*, which she describes as "the first album I got as a youngster that made me say, 'Whoa!'" She also loves Aretha Franklin's two-album set, *Amazing Grace,* and Nancy Wilson's *All My Heart*. "I think they are the epitome of artists," she comments. "They can still belt out a song and make you cry or belt out a song and make you laugh and shout."

HOBBIES AND OTHER INTERESTS

When she has some free time, Adams heads to the golf course. In addition to playing golf with her husband, she enjoys running.

RECORDINGS

Just As I Am, 1987
Through the Storm, 1991

Save the World, 1993
More Than a Melody, 1995
Yolanda . . . Live in Washington, 1996
Songs from the Heart, 1998
*Mountain High . . . Valley Low,*1999
Christmas With Yolanda Adams, 2000
The Experience, 2001
Believe, 2001

SELECTED HONORS AND AWARDS

Stellar Awards (Stellar Awards Gospel Music Academy): 1992, Best Female
  Contemporary Gospel Artist, for *Through the Storm;* 1994 (three awards),
  Song of the Year, for "The Battle is the Lord's", Contemporary Album of
  the Year, for *Save the World,* Best Traditional Female Solo Performance,
  for "The Battle is the Lord's"; 1996, Female Vocalist of the Year, for
  Yolanda . . . Live in Washington; 2001 (five awards), Artist of the Year,
  Female Vocalist of the Year, CD of the Year, Contemporary Female
  Vocalist of the Year (all for *Mountain High . . . Valley Low*), Music Video of
  the Year, for "Open My Heart"
Dove Awards (Gospel Music Association): 1992 (two awards), Best
  Traditional Gospel Album, for *Through the Storm,* Best Traditional Gospel
  Song, for "Through the Storm"; 1999, Traditional Gospel Recorded Song
  of the Year, for "Is Your All on the Altar?"
Soul Train Music Awards: 1995, Best Gospel Album, for *More Than a
  Melody;* 2001, Best Female R&B/Soul Single, for "Open My Heart"
Image Awards (NAACP): 2000, Best Contemporary Gospel Artist, for
  Mountain High . . . Valley Low; 2001 (four awards), Outstanding
  Performance in a Variety Series/Special, for "Soul Train Lady of Soul
  Awards," Outstanding Song, Outstanding Female Artist, Outstanding
  Contemporary Gospel Artist (all for "Open My Heart"); 2002,
  Outstanding Contemporary Gospel Artist, for *Believe*
Grammy Awards: 2000, Best Contemporary Soul Gospel Album, for
  Mountain High . . . Valley Low; 2002, Best Contemporary Soul Gospel
  Album, for *The Experience*
American Music Award: 2002, for Favorite Contemporary Inspirational
  Artist
Lady of Soul Award (Soul Train): 2002, Best Gospel Album, for *Believe*
Gospel Music Excellence Award (Gospel Music Workshop of America):
  2002, Female Vocalist of the Year, Urban Contemporary, for "Never Give
  Up"
Best Gospel Artist (Black Entertainment Television): 2002

FURTHER READING

Books

Contemporary Black Biography, Vol. 17, 1998
Contemporary Musicians, Vol. 23, 1999
Who's Who among African Americans, 2002

Periodicals

Chicago Tribune, Dec. 24, 1995, p.2
Current Biography Yearbook, 2002
Detroit Free Press, Dec. 10, 1999, p.D1
Ebony, Aug. 2000, p.42; May 2001, p.58
Essence, July. 2001, p.106
Jet, June 12, 2000, p.55; Feb. 5, 2001, p.61
Today's Christian Woman, Sep.-Oct. 2002, p.94
Washington Post, Feb. 11, 2000, p.NO8

Online Database

Biography Resource Center Online, 2003, articles from *Contemporary Black Biography,* 1998, and *Contemporary Musicians,* 1999

ADDRESS

Yolanda Adams
Elektra Entertainment Group
75 Rockefeller Plaza
New York, NY 10019

E-mail: yolanda@yolandaadams.org

WORLD WIDE WEB SITES

http://www.yolandaadams.org
http://www.elektra.com/elektra/yolandaadams/index.jhtml

Laura Bush 1946-

American Librarian and Literacy Activist
First Lady of the United States

BIRTH

Laura Bush was born Laura Welch on November 4, 1946, in
Midland, Texas. Her father, Harold, was a homebuilder who
owned his own contracting business, and her mother, Jenna,
was the company's bookkeeper. Laura is an only child.

YOUTH

Jenna Welch remembers that her daughter "was just born a
nice quiet little kiddo." She started reading to Laura "from the

time she could open her eyes." To this day, reading with her mother is one of Laura Bush's fondest childhood memories. Her favorite books included the "Little House" series by Laura Ingalls Wilder, in part because she and the heroine shared the same first name, "but what I loved even more was sitting with my mother, listening to her read." She also loved "Nancy Drew" mysteries by Carolyn Keene and *Little Women* by Louisa May Alcott.

Laura and her mother made frequent trips to the local public library, which was housed in the Midland County Courthouse. She still remembers the effect it had on her. "These trips to the library were a defining part of my childhood. Even at three and four years of age, I remember thinking how special the library must be. Here were so many books with people of all ages enjoying them, located in the most important building in our town."

——— **"** ———

"These trips to the library were a defining part of my childhood. Even at three and four years of age, I remember thinking how special the li- brary must be. Here were so many books with people of all ages enjoying them, locat- ed in the most important building in our town."

——— **"** ———

In addition to reading, Bush enjoyed church and church activities, Brownies and Girl Scouts, and playing with friends. She particularly liked playing school. She'd line up her dolls as if they were in a classroom and "teach" them to read. "In a lot of ways, I had a perfect childhood," she told a reporter in 2000. "We felt very free to do what- ever we wanted. You could ride your bike downtown, go to the Rexall Drug and get a ham sandwich for lunch. But at the same time, we were shel- tered."

Midland is a middle-class town in west Texas, where many families made their living in the oil business. One of those was the family of George W. Bush. Yet even though they grew up in the same town, and even went to the same junior high, Laura Welch and George W. Bush didn't meet grow- ing up or in school. They weren't officially introduced until they were adults.

EDUCATION

Laura Welch went to James Bowie Elementary School in Midland, where she was an excellent student. She especially loved her second grade teacher and credits her with the inspiration to become a teacher herself. Laura went on to Midland Junior High and Midland High School. An otherwise happy high school career was marred by tragedy in her junior year when she was involved in a fatal traffic accident. She was driving a car and ran a stop sign, hitting a car driven by a high school friend. The young man died in the accident. The boy's family never blamed her or brought charges against her, but it remains a difficult and painful memory.

After graduating from Midland High in 1964, Bush went to Southern Methodist University in Dallas, Texas. She studied education, receiving her bachelor's degree in 1968.

First Lady Laura Bush with her mother, Jenna Welch

CAREER HIGHLIGHTS

Over the next ten years, Bush worked in elementary schools, first as a teacher and then as a librarian. She devoted herself to causes that she continues to champion today as First Lady: early childhood education and the importance of reading to learning.

Bush's first teaching job was at Longfellow Elementary School in Dallas, Texas. After a year of teaching at Longfellow, she took a job at John F. Kennedy Elementary in Houston, Texas. One of her former students remembers that "the kids really did love her. She'd go outside and play with us. If you had problems on reading and spelling, she'd take a little more time with you." She taught at Kennedy for several years, then decided she wanted to become a librarian. She went back to school, this time to the University of Texas at Austin, where she studied for a library science degree. She graduated in 1973 with her M.L.S. — Master's of Library Science.

Bush's first job as a librarian was in Houston, where she worked at a branch of the Houston Public Library. The next year, she returned to Austin, where she worked as the librarian at Dawson Elementary School, a job she held for three years.

MARRIAGE AND FAMILY

In the summer of 1977, Laura Welch met George W. Bush at the home of mutual friends in Midland, Texas. (Because of the confusion of names, the son is usually referred to as George W. Bush, while his father is called George Herbert Walker Bush, or just George Bush. For more information on Laura's husband, George W. Bush, see *Biography Today*, Sep. 2000, and Updates in the Annual Cumulations for 2000, 2001, and 2002; for more information on his father, George Bush, see *Biography Today*, Jan. 1992.)

Laura's friends had been trying to get the two together for years, but she was a bit reluctant. She knew his background, with a father who was a prominent Republican politician. In 1977, George W. Bush was running for office, too, for a spot on the Texas legislature. She thought he sounded "too political," she laughingly recalls. George W. Bush remembers their meeting well, claiming it was "love at first sight." For her part, Laura remembers he was a lot of fun and had a great sense of humor. But the future President was also persistent, and they quickly hit it off. They dated for just three months before marrying in November 1977. Their twin daughters, Jenna and Barbara, were born in 1981.

EARLY POLITICAL CAMPAIGNS

When Laura and George W. Bush married, she made him promise she would never have to make a political speech for him. But just months after their wedding, she was up on a stage, speaking at a political rally for her husband. With sly humor, she told the audience about his pledge and explained her appearance on his behalf: "So much for political promises." Bush didn't win that first election, but he learned a lot about politics that he put to use in later races.

Over the next several years George W. Bush headed an oil company, while Laura Bush devoted herself to raising her daughters and volunteering at the girls' school and at the local library. She also helped her husband quit drinking. George W. Bush has acknowledged that he had a problem with alcohol. He has said that he decided to quit drinking because he was "a high-energy person, and alcohol began competing with my ability to keep up my energy level." Some people have claimed that Laura greatly influenced his decision, but she won't take the credit. She says he's a disciplined man who did it on his own.

In 1987, the family moved to Washington, D.C. Bush's father, George Herbert Walker Bush, had served as Ronald Reagan's vice president from 1980 to 1988, and was running for President. George W. became one of his father's closest advisers. In 1988, George Bush was elected President, and George W. and his family moved back to Texas. From 1988 to 1994, Bush was a managing partner of the Texas Rangers baseball team, headquar-

*George W. Bush campaigning for a seat in the Texas legislature
with his wife, Laura Bush, 1978.*

tered outside of Dallas. Laura and the girls attended many baseball games, and as Jenna and Barbara got older, Laura became more involved in library and literacy programs.

In 1994, George W. Bush announced his re-entry into politics. He decided to take on popular Texas governor Ann Richards. Laura Bush wasn't pleased. She was concerned about the effect on her family of the close press scrutiny that goes along with politics. She wanted to protect their privacy, particularly for her daughters, who were just 13 years old. She'd also lived through the tough times the press had given her father-in-law, George Bush, when he'd lost his re-election bid in 1992.

Despite her reservations, Laura Bush proved to be an able and intuitive campaigner. She has often been described as quiet and reserved, but she's also candid with her husband. On the campaign trail, George asked her what she thought of a speech he'd just given. "Well, it wasn't that good," she told him, after which he drove into the garage wall. He has often called her his "rock," a source of strength, but also someone who can rein him in when he gets a little too volatile.

FIRST LADY OF TEXAS

George W. Bush won the Texas governor's race in 1994, and the family moved to the state capital in Austin. As First Lady of Texas, Laura Bush had a statewide forum for the causes she believed in so deeply. She began a literacy campaign aimed at whole families, so that not just children, but parents and grandparents too, could learn to read together. She started organizations to help parents help children get ready for school. One of the main themes of Bush's career has been that reading readiness is perhaps the most important indicator of a child's success in school. She believes that children need to be read to from infancy. The more they are read to, the more they'll be able to recognize words, word patterns, and all aspects that go into reading.

> "I've never been that interested in clothes," Bush said in response to media criticism of the way she dressed. She was really comfortable in "jeans, pants, T-shirts," and wasn't embarrassed about buying her makeup at the drug store. "I can take scrutiny or criticism of how I look with a grain of salt because I think there are things more important than how I look or wear my hair."

In 1998, Laura Bush helped write and promote a bill that provided $17 million for early childhood development programs, with increased funding going to established programs like Head Start. She worked with other governors' wives on women's health initiatives. She helped to create "Rainbow Rooms" for Texas children, which provide clothing and other important necessities to children who have been abused and neglected. She also helped raise money for breast cancer research and for art preservation.

In 1996, Bush started the Texas Book Fair, an annual celebration of books, authors, and reading that has raised more than $1 million for Texas libraries. Among people from both political parties, Laura Bush became known as one of the finest First Ladies in Texas history. She continued to pursue her interests in her typical low-key way. At the same time, she did her best to guard her children's privacy and assure them a normal adolescence. She was firm with the press in how they were to treat her daughters. She asked that they not be photographed or interviewed, and that they be left alone by the media. The media generally did as they were asked, but some were not above criticizing the way Laura Bush looked or

A family portrait on the rocks in Kennebunkport, Maine, 1987.
Left to right: Jenna, George W., Laura, and Barbara.

the way she dressed. That really didn't bother her. "I've never been that interested in clothes," she says. She was really comfortable in "jeans, pants, T-shirts," and wasn't embarrassed about buying her makeup at the drug store. "I can take scrutiny or criticism of how I look with a grain of salt because I think there are things more important than how I look or wear my hair."

THE ROAD TO THE WHITE HOUSE

In 1999, George W. Bush announced that he would seek the nomination to become the Republican candidate for President. Laura Bush traveled around the United States, campaigning for her husband. She attended and gave speeches at political rallies all around the country. She spoke at the 2000 Republican Convention, giving many Americans their first glimpse of the woman who would later become First Lady. The election of 2000 turned out to be one of the most hotly contested in years, and for over a month after the vote it was unclear who had actually won. It wasn't until De-

First Lady Laura Bush with her daughters, Barbara and Jenna, at the inauguration of President George W. Bush, January 2001.

cember that the results were finally determined, and George W. Bush became the 43rd President of the United States. The day the election results were announced, Laura Bush was still busy with her work as the First Lady of Texas, chairing a meeting on that year's Texas Book Fair even as her husband got ready to give his acceptance speech.

FIRST LADY OF THE UNITED STATES

In January 2001, Laura Bush moved to Washington, D.C., and into the White House. Once again, she used her position as First Lady to promote the causes she believes in so passionately: reading initiatives and early childhood education. She launched new programs, including one to recruit teachers and to make sure children start school ready to learn.

THE TRAGEDY OF SEPTEMBER 11TH

Then, on September 11, 2001, the world of Laura Bush, and of all U.S. citizens, changed dramatically. On that day, terrorists attacked the United States. Hijackers forced two commercial airplanes to crash into the twin towers of the World Trade Center in New York City. Less than an hour later, hijackers forced a plane to crash into the Pentagon, the home of the Department of Defense in Washington, D.C. The damage to the World

Trade Center was devastating. An hour after the attack, the twin towers collapsed. Almost 3,000 people died in New York. At the Pentagon, the death toll reached 184.

Later, it was learned that there were also terrorists on board a fourth plane. But passengers on that plane fought back and prevented the terrorists from carrying out their plans. The plane crashed in an empty field in Pennsylvania without hitting any other inhabited area or symbolic buildings. It was later conjectured that the plane that crashed in Pennsylvania was headed to another target in Washington, possibly the U.S. Capitol building.

Laura Bush was in the U.S. Capitol building that morning, about to give a speech to Congress on early childhood development. When news of the attack came, she was taken back to the White House, where she waited for news from her husband, who was out of town. When he finally landed in Washington several hours later, they both made an important decision. Against the recommendations of their advisers, they decided to stay in the White House, and not to move to a secret location.

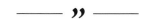

"The most comforting people I've been with since September 11 are the second graders I've read to. Children who are seven and eight years old have a wonderful outlook on life. They know what's important."

Within hours of the attack, federal officials stated that they thought the terrorists were acting under the direction of Osama bin Laden. (For more information on bin Laden, see *Biography Today,* April 2002.) Bin Laden is a Saudi Arabian extremist who has been linked to other terrorist attacks against the U.S. He is reported to have financed and planned the 1993 attack on the World Trade Center. That attack killed six and injured several hundred. He is also considered to be behind the bombing of U.S. embassies in Kenya and Tanzania in 1998. And he is linked to the attack on the U.S.S. Cole, a Navy ship that was bombed in 2000 while in Yemen. Whether bin Laden is still alive is unknown, but the U.S. continues to pursue him and the worldwide terrorist network Al Qaeda. The U.S. is focusing its military actions on finding and destroying Al-Qaeda terrorist cells throughout the Middle East, Asia, and all over the world.

In the days after the terrorist attacks, Laura Bush became a constant and calming presence in the country. She appeared at the disaster sites, where she comforted the families who had lost loved ones and thanked the many rescue workers. She went to schools all over the country to meet with children and talk to them. She wanted to assure them that they were safe, and that their parents and teachers cared for them. They made her feel better, too. "The most comforting people I've been with since September 11 are the second graders I've read to," she said. "Children who are seven and eight years old have a wonderful outlook on life. They know what's important." In November 2001, Laura Bush became the only First Lady to give the weekly presidential radio broadcast. She spoke out against the oppression of women and children under the Taliban regime in Afghanistan.

——— *"* ———

"Children and teachers need library resources — especially books — and the expertise of a librarian to succeed. Books, information technology, and school librarians who are part of the schools' professional team are basic ingredients for student achievement."

——— *"* ———

Laura Bush's new, more visible role as what has been called "Caretaker in Chief" was warmly embraced by a grieving nation. And she returned to her role as an enthusiastic champion of education. She appeared before Congress again in January 2002, outlining her concern that preschool children get the help they need to get ready for reading and learning in school. She also encouraged more adults to get involved in their communities as mentors.

PROMOTING LIBRARIES AND LITERACY

In June 2002, Bush held a White House conference on school libraries, unveiling a $5 million federal funding initiative. "School libraries help teachers teach and children learn," she said. "Children and teachers need library resources — especially books — and the expertise of a librarian to succeed. Books, information technology, and school librarians who are part of the schools' professional team are basic ingredients for student achievement."

In July 2002, she started the Laura Bush Foundation for America's Libraries. Its purpose is to enhance the collections in school libraries by providing grants to allow libraries to buy additional books. "My lifelong passion for books began when I was a little girl. This new Foundation provides yet another opportunity to share with America's children the magical world of books and reading," Bush said. "A love of books, of holding a book, turning its pages, looking at its pictures, and living its fascinating stories goes

First Lady Laura Bush reads a book to Big Bird, Elmo, and friends on "Sesame Street."

hand-in-hand with a love of learning. Every child in America should have access to a well-stocked school or community library. . . . An investment in libraries is an investment in our children's future."

BOOK FESTIVALS IN WASHINGTON

Bush had actually started a new reading initiative in Washington on the eve of September 11. On September 8, 2001, she launched the first annual National Book Festival at the Library of Congress. She invited more than 50 famous authors to read their works to people in a weekend celebration of books and authors. Inspired by the Texas Book Fair, the National Book Festival drew more than 30,000 people in its first year, and even more in 2002.

Bush also started another series of book-related events. She invited authors from all over the country to come to the White House for symposiums on

————— " —————

*"A love of books,
of holding a book,
turning its pages,
looking at its pictures, and
living its fascinating stories
goes hand-in-hand
with a love of learning.
Every child in America
should have access to a
well-stocked school or
community library. . . . An
investment in libraries
is an investment in our
children's future."*

————— " —————

American literature. So far, writers have attended series devoted to Mark Twain, the Harlem Renaissance, and American women writers of the West. Bush invited people from across the political spectrum, including several who disagreed strongly with the President's political stand on various issues. Some of these writers were surprised to be invited to the White House, because their political beliefs were so different from those of the Bush administration. But Laura Bush claimed that "There's nothing political about American literature," and the discussions inspired by the series were lively and far-reaching.

But the series came to a temporary halt in January 2003 when the First Lady postponed a planned symposium on the poetry of Emily Dickinson, Langston Hughes, and Walt Whitman. She had invited several poets who were disturbed at the Bush administration's proposed military action in Iraq. These poets planned to use the conference to protest President Bush's stance and to express their own political views. At this point the series is on hold, and a new date has not been set. Regardless of the future of the poetry symposium, Laura Bush will surely continue to promote reading and literacy through her role as First Lady.

HOBBIES AND OTHER INTERESTS

In her spare time, Bush still loves to read. She also likes to garden at the Bush's ranch in Crawford, Texas. She enjoys taking the family dogs, Barney and Spot, for walks on the ranch and at Camp David, a presidential retreat in the Maryland countryside.

FURTHER READING

Books

Anderson, Christopher. *George and Laura: Portrait of an American Marriage,* 2002
Watson, Robert P. *American First Ladies,* 2002

Periodicals

American Libraries, Feb. 2001, p.50; Oct. 2001, p.16
Austin-American, Sep. 29, 1996, p.E1
Current Biography Yearbook, 2001
Good Housekeeping, Jan. 2002, p.100
Library Journal, Oct. 2001, p.11
New York Times, Oct. 7, 2002, p.A1; Oct. 10, 2002, p.A34; Jan. 31, 2003
New York Times Magazine, Sep. 9, 2001, p.61
Newsday, Jan. 3, 2001, p.B6
Newsweek, Nov. 22, 1999, p.42; Sep. 27, 2001, p.69; Oct. 8, 2001, p.33
People, Oct. 9, 2000, p.64; May 14, 2001, p.159; Jan. 29, 2001, p.50; Jan. 21, 2002, p.84
Psychology Today, Dec. 2002, p.34
Publishers Weekly, Oct. 21, 2001, p.12
Texas Monthly, Nov. 1966, p.120; Apr. 2001, p.80
Time, Jan. 8, 2001, p.32
U.S. News and World Report, Sep. 10, 2001
Washington Post, June 15, 2001, p.C1

Other

"Morning Edition," National Public Radio Transcript, Sep. 4, 2001; Sep. 17, 2001
"Weekend Edition," National Public Radio Transcript, July 30, 2000

Online Database

Biography Resource Center Online, 2003

ADDRESS

Laura Bush
The Office of the First Lady
The White House
1600 Pennsylvania Ave.
Washington, D.C. 20500

WORLD WIDE WEB SITES

http://www.whitehouse.gov/firstlady
http://www.laurabushfoundation.org

Eminem 1972 -

American Rap Artist and Songwriter
Creator of *The Slim Shady LP*, *The Marshall Mathers LP*, and *The Eminem Show*
Star of the Hit Film *8 Mile*

BIRTH

Eminem was born Marshall Bruce Mathers III on October 17, 1972, in Kansas City, Missouri. Although he is known professionally by the name Eminem, his friends call him Marshall or Em. His mother, Debbie Nelson, was 17 when he was born. She left his father less than a year later. She has worked off and on as a caregiver, cosmetologist, waitress, receptionist, and taxi-service operator. His father, Marshall Bruce Mathers II, a steelworker, has never been part of his son's life. Eminem said, "I never knew him. Never even seen a picture of him." Eminem has one younger half-brother, Nathan.

YOUTH

The anger that fuels Eminem's brilliant raps came straight from his tough childhood. He and his mother moved constantly and got by on a small, unsteady income. "I don't like to give the sob story: growing up in a single-parent home, never knew my father, my mother never worked, and when friends came over I'd hide the welfare cheese," he said. "It's like the real, stereotypical, trailer-park white trash."

Eminem spent his early life in South Dakota, his father's native state. When he was about two, his mother left him in the care of a great aunt in Missouri. His mother reclaimed him when he was five, and for the next seven years they bounced between Missouri and the Detroit area. He attended 15 to 20 schools during that time. "We just kept moving back and forth because my mother never had a job. We kept getting kicked out of every house we were in," Eminem said. "I believe six months was the longest we ever lived in a house."

"I don't like to give the sob story: growing up in a single-parent home, never knew my father, my mother never worked, and when friends came over I'd hide the welfare cheese," Eminem said. "It's like the real, stereotypical, trailer-park white trash."

From the time he was about 12, Eminem and his mother remained in the Detroit area. But they continued to move constantly. They drifted between run-down neighborhoods in the city of Detroit and the gritty, blue-collar suburbs just northeast of it. The city was mostly African-American, and the suburbs mostly white. A busy street called 8 Mile Road was the boundary between the two. According to Eminem, "It's the borderline of what separates suburbs from city. It's the color line. I grew up on both sides of it and saw everything," he said. "I had [white] friends who had racist redneck fathers and stepfathers. I had black friends. It's just American culture." When it was time to title his debut film about a white guy crossing the color divide into black rap music, *8 Mile* was a natural choice.

Whatever neighborhood he landed in, Eminem found it hard to fit in. He tried to lose himself in television and comic books. At one time he even wanted to be a comic-book artist. But he couldn't hide from the school bullies. Small for his age and forever the new kid, he got picked on a lot— he ticked people off with his smart-aleck attitude. In his song "Brain Damage" on *The Slim Shady LP*, he describes himself as "A kid who refused to respect adults/Wore spectacles with taped frames and a freckled nose/A corny lookin' white boy, scrawny and always ornery/'Cause I was always sick of brawny bullies pickin' on me." The song is based on the worst bullying he ever suffered, when he was nine. An older boy beat Eminem until he was unconscious. His hearing and vision were affected, and he spent 10 days in the hospital.

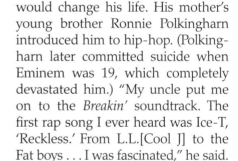

In his song "Brain Damage" on **The Slim Shady LP,** *he describes himself as "A kid who refused to respect adults/Wore spectacles with taped frames and a freckled nose/A corny lookin' white boy, scrawny and always ornery/'Cause I was always sick of brawny bullies pickin' on me."*

About the same time as the attack, Eminem first heard the music that would change his life. His mother's young brother Ronnie Polkingharn introduced him to hip-hop. (Polkingharn later committed suicide when Eminem was 19, which completely devastated him.) "My uncle put me on to the *Breakin'* soundtrack. The first rap song I ever heard was Ice-T, 'Reckless.' From L.L.[Cool J] to the Fat boys . . . I was fascinated," he said. "When L.L. first came out with 'I'm Bad,' I wanted to do it, to rhyme. Standing in front of the mirror, I wanted to be like L.L." Over time, Eminem and his uncle, who were close in age, moved on to more hardcore gangsta rappers like N.W.A. and 2-Live Crew. Gangsta rap sprang from urban African-American ghettoes. Full of graphic language and violent images, gangsta rap often denigrates women and portrays other men as rivals to be destroyed. Eminem found it irresistible. "Like about 14 years old . . . I first decided to become a hot rapper," he said.

Rap became an outlet for Eminem's frustrations. The family's financial troubles were constant. His mother was neglectful and manipulative. He had a hard time getting along with her, and their relationship got worse as he got older. "You couldn't even understand how crazy it was," said Proof, a close childhood friend. "He got kicked out of his house so much, I stayed there more than he did." School was another difficulty. Eminem was enrolled at Lincoln High School in Warren, a suburb of Detroit. But he skipped a lot of classes and failed ninth grade twice. A former high-school classmate said Eminem stood out only for his skill at rapping and rhyme. He got attention rapping against others in the school lunchroom, and he also gave a rousing performance at a school talent show. In 1989, he dropped out for good. In 1999 he said, "I tried to go back to school five years ago, but I couldn't do it. I just wanted to rap and be a star."

FIRST JOBS

Like Jimmy "Rabbit" Smith in the movie *8 Mile,* Eminem pursued his dream of hip-hop stardom with seriousness and purpose. But he had to earn money in the meantime. He held a series of low-paying jobs while he practiced rapping. For several years in the mid-1990s, he worked as a cook and dishwasher at a family restaurant in an eastside suburb of Detroit. His co-workers remember him as a funny, friendly guy who rapped out the food orders. And they noticed how diligent he was about his music. "I had to tell him to turn down the radio occasionally, but overall he was one of the better cooks we had," said his former boss. "We're all very happy for [his success]. I know he worked hard for it."

CAREER HIGHLIGHTS

After he dropped out of school, Eminem threw himself into composing rhymes and rapping. He developed a habit he keeps to this day — filling sheets of paper with tiny, almost unreadable lines as he worked out the best rhymes. A notorious perfectionist, he works his material over and over again until he is satisfied. During this period, he began to call himself "M&M" — a play on his initials. (His manager later convinced him to re-spell it.) He also got up his nerve to enter rapping battles at Detroit night clubs. These contests, known as freestyle, pitted one rapper against another to see who could spew out the fastest, most outrageous insults in the cleverest rhymes. A skinny, blue-eyed white kid was an unlikely sight in these venues. The vast majority of the contestants and audiences were African-American, and Eminem had to be quick to win their respect. He developed a coping strategy that he still uses: he'd joke about his own flaws and weaknesses before his critics could. Not only was it hilarious, but it stymied his opponents.

Breaking In

In 1990, Eminem got his first break. A young Detroit-area music producer named Mark Bass heard him rap on an open-mike radio program in De-

troit. Bass called the station and invited Eminem to his FBT Productions studio for an impromptu audition. Eminem turned up at 4 a.m. Before long, Mark Bass and his brother Jeff began to record some cuts with Eminem. He was then a rough-edged teenager who was just developing his style, according to Mark Bass. His rhymes weren't out of the ordinary, "but his rhythm was fantastic. It always reminded me of a drum solo, suddenly going in a different direction in the middle of a lick. And you understood what he was saying—the enunciation was incredible."

In 1996, Mark and Jeff Bass borrowed $1,500 from their mother to produce 1,000 copies of Eminem's first recording, *Infinite*, under their Web Enter-tainment label. "*Infinite* was me trying to figure out how I wanted my rap style to be, how I wanted to sound on the mic [microphone] and present myself," Eminem said. "It was a growing stage." He placed high hopes on the record—and not just to satisfy his ego. He and his longtime girlfriend, Kim Scott, had had a daughter on Christmas Day 1995. (He and Kim later married and divorced). He needed money to support the baby, Hailie Jade. But the album sold only a handful of copies. And Eminem got little credit for his rapping. "I caught a lot of flak: 'You're trying to sound like AZ. You're trying to sound like Nas. You're trying to sound like somebody from New York. And you're white. You shouldn't rap. You should go into rock-and-roll.' . . . That started pissing me off. And I started releasing that anger in the songs." These songs became eight cuts on his next release, *The Slim Shady EP.*

——— *"* ———

Creating the Slim Shady Character

On *The Slim Shady EP* (1997), Eminem created a character who has become a fixture on all of his albums: his vile, outrageous alter-ego, Slim Shady. Shady is a drug-taking, law-breaking, woman-abusing, foul-mouthed rap monster. He rants about the real-life figures in Eminem's life—everyone from his girlfriend Kim, to his mother, to people on Detroit's music scene. He doesn't hesitate to blast them by name. Eminem described Slim Shady as "the evil side of me, the sarcastic, foul-mouthed side of me." According to Eminem, the character let him vent his anger—and pour more feeling and creativity into his rapping. "[The] more I started writing and the more I slipped into this Slim Shady character, the more it just started becoming me," he said. "My true feelings were coming out and I just needed an outlet to dump them in. I needed some type of persona. I needed an excuse to let go of all this rage, this dark humor, the pain, and the happiness." Unlike his earlier release, Eminem saw *The Slim Shady EP* as a record to please himself—and no one else. The material "brought more of my personality in," he said. "That's when I found myself."

When Eminem was starting out, says producer Mark Bass, his rhymes weren't out of the ordinary, "but his rhythm was fantastic. It always reminded me of a drum solo, suddenly going in a different direction in the middle of a lick. And you understood what he was saying—the enunciation was incredible."

——— *"* ———

Eminem's creativity was flourishing. But real life still dogged him. He had been fired from the restaurant. He was completely broke and discouraged. But he was about to get the break that launched his career. With help from a magazine journalist who liked his Slim Shady cuts, he won a spot to compete at *Rap Sheet* magazine's 1997 "Rap Olympics." This major freestyle competition in Los Angeles was an important showcase for talent—and carried a first prize of $1,5000 that Eminem badly needed. He battled furiously for an hour, toppling every opponent. He rhymed brilliantly, hurling back every insult thrown at him about his race. Then in a slip-up, he missed first place. He was furious. But though he didn't win the competition, he grabbed the interest of an intern from Interscope Records. Eminem got noticed for his distinctive, nasal-sounding voice, his complex rhythms, and his clear enunciation. The outrageous content of his lyrics grabbed attention, too. And so did his race.

Slim Shady is "the evil side of me, the sarcastic, foul-mouthed side of me," according to Eminem. "[The] more I started writing and the more I slipped into this Slim Shady character, the more it just started becoming me. My true feelings were coming out and I just needed an outlet to dump them in. I needed some type of persona. I needed an excuse to let go of all this rage, this dark humor, the pain, and the happiness."

His Rap Olympics performance won him a slot on an influential Los Angeles radio program. "The Wake Up Show" with DJs Sway and Tech was a major rap showcase. "I felt like, 'It's my time to shine. I have to rip this,'" Eminem said. "At that time, I felt like it was a life-or-death situation." He unleashed a savage stream of lyrics that amazed the DJs and the audience. The feat won him the 1997 Wake Up Show Freestyle Performer of the Year. His underground record "5 Star Generals" caught notice in Japan, New York, and Los Angeles. He also won a place performing on a national rap tour.

At the same time, the intern from Interscope Records passed *The Slim Shady EP* to producer Jimmy Iovine. Iovine placed it in the hands of performer and producer Andre Young. Better known as Dr. Dre, he founded the rap groups N.W.A. and The Chronic. Dr. Dre is renowned and respected as a godfather of gangsta rap. And he wanted to sign Eminem to his label. "Growing up, I was one of the biggest fans of N.W.A., from putting on the sunglasses and looking in the mirror and lip-synching to wanting to be Dr. Dre, to be Ice Cube," Eminem said. "This is the biggest hip-hop producer ever." For Dr. Dre, race was no issue in signing Eminem. "You know, he's got blue eyes, he's a white kid," said Dr. Dre. "But I don't give a [care] if you're purple. If you can kick it, I'm working with you."

The Slim Shady LP

Taking to the recording studio, Dre and Eminem hit it off immediately. In the first six hours of working together they recorded four songs. "[Messin'] with the best producer in hip-hop music, I had to be more on point," Eminem said. "When I got in the studio with him, I had to show him something extra. . . . I had to be *extra*." Three of their initial cuts made it to *The Slim Shady LP*: "Guilty Conscience," "Role Model," and the hit single "My Name Is." All three songs trashed the notion of celebrities and other adults as shining examples for youth. In "Role Model," Eminem attacked then-President Bill Clinton with the line, "If I said I never did drugs/that would mean I lie and get [sex] even more than the president does." Many of the songs contained irreverence for public figures and colleagues in the music business. In addition, he often used dark humor that targeted Eminem himself—making him what the *New York Times* called "hip-hop's first self-mocking anti-hero." He often played his race for laughs, using his Midwestern twang to emphasize his white-boy geekiness.

The lyrical content of *The Slim Shady LP* set the tone for the future. Eminem was apparently playing a character or a role—although it's impossible to tell when he's speaking as Slim Shady and when he's speaking as himself. From his recording, it's impossible to tell what Eminem really believes. *The Slim Shady LP* demonstrates his talent as a charismatic, gifted wordsmith. Many of the rhymes are clever and even funny. As Eminem said, "The kids listening to my music get the joke. They can tell when I'm serious and when I'm not. They can tell the entertainment of it." But others weren't so sure.

The songs on *The Slim Shady LP* are filled with hate, self-loathing, and violence. He expresses a lot of hate toward his ex-wife Kim, his mother, women in general, and homosexuals. He calls women bitches, sluts, and worse; he calls homosexuals faggots. His language offended many people, although Eminem claimed that wasn't his intent. For example, as he told Kurt Loder of MTV, "'Faggot' to me doesn't necessarily mean gay people. 'Faggot' to me just means . . . taking away your manhood. You're a sissy. You're a coward. . . . So, when I started saying 'faggot' on record, I started getting people going, 'You have something against gay people' and I thought it was funny, because I don't." Throughout the record, the songs are riddled with swear words and rants about drugs. The album also includes disturbing images about people close to Eminem. "My Name Is" rips into his mother for drug-taking and neglect. "97 Bonnie and Clyde," in which he fantasizes about killing his wife, includes the gurgling voice of his daughter, Hailie, then aged three. The rapper imagines a father-daughter outing to dump the body of the child's murdered mother in a lake: "There goes Mommy splashing in the water/ No more fighting with dad, no more restraining order." So while critics and audiences enjoyed his rhythm and dazzling, lightening-quick rhymes, many struggled to come to terms with the offensive nature of his lyrics.

The Slim Shady LP was released in 1998, and it debuted on the *Billboard* magazine album chart at No. 3. The record went on to sell more than four million copies. Eminem won two Grammy Awards, for Best Rap Solo Performance (for "My Name Is") and Best Rap Album. But as the acclaim rained down, so did criticism. Music executives and advocates for women and homosexuals attacked Eminem for his material [see the sidebar entitled "Eminem's Changing Reputation," pages 46–47]. He was also targeted during his tour in the spring of 1999. Many criticized his lackluster performances—some as brief as 25 minutes. Typically, Eminem shot back in songs, which he released on his second major album.

——— **"** ———

"Rap, overall, is entertainment. I'm trying to bring it in an entertaining way that's clever—you never know what's going to come, what I'm going to say next. I try to catch people off guard with punch lines. I catch myself off guard a lot of times when I'm writing."

——— **"** ———

The Marshall Mathers LP

Eminem released *The Marshall Mathers LP* in 2000. He said his own favorite song from the album is "The Way I Am," which he called "a message to everybody to get off my back." The album is also a furious assault not only on his mother, his wife, and homosexuals, but also on a string of celebrities whom the rapper insults personally. He addresses the critics of his first album, including the hypocrites of middle America: in "Who Knew," he scorns parents who complain about his lyrics, but let their kids freely watch violent movies.

But *The Marshall Mathers LP* was more than a revenge rant. The beats are seductive, and the wordplay is as brilliant as ever. Beneath the rage and profanity, listeners found material that was intelligent and ironic. "After *The Marshall Mathers LP* I upgraded everything. Flow, rhyme, character, and the whole shebang," Eminem said. Many noted that Eminem had polished his skill as a storyteller. The hit "Stan" creates a vivid picture of a fan

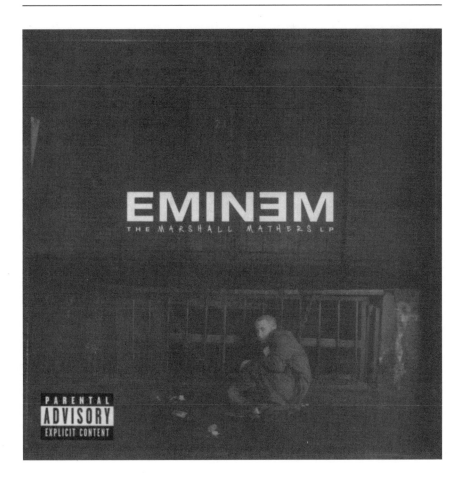

obsessed with Slim Shady. After Shady ignores his fan letters, Stan kills his pregnant girlfriend and commits suicide. Played against a song-sample by pop singer, Dido, the song tells a tale that is shocking, funny, and poignant, all at once. "Kim" recounts a murderous argument between Eminem and his wife as their then-five-year-old daughter looks on. Such songs often have Eminem acting out several characters' voices. And the stories are propelled by rapid-fire background remarks. These side comments are like sound balloons in a comic strip that comment on the main action of the story.

In his introduction to Eminem's book, *Angry Blonde*, Jonathan Schecter noted Eminem's skill for painting scenes: "Em's active imagination turns records into mini movies featuring multiple characters and cartoonish ad-lib tracks. Recurring figures such as Ken Kaniff, Kim, and now Stan create

Eminem's Changing Reputation

Beginning with the release of *The Slim Shady LP*, Eminem has come under a barrage of criticism for corrupting young audiences. *Billboard Magazine* editor Timothy White wrote an entire article denouncing his lyrics. They are "violent and inflammatory," White said, accusing Eminem of "exploiting the world's misery." Not long afterward, Lynne Cheney, the wife of the U.S. vice president, testified before Congress that Eminem promoted the worst forms of violence against women. Her comments were echoed by Kim Gandy, the executive vice president of the National Organization for Women. "Offensiveness is not the issue," she said. "I think [his music] is actually dangerous to girls and women." The authorities at the Gay and Lesbian Alliance Against Defamation (GLAAD) called his lyrics "the most hateful, homophobic, and violence-encouraging we have ever seen." Yet these charges didn't seem to affect his popularity, his record sales, or his appeal to young listeners.

Controversy about Eminem continued in June 2002, when he got in trouble with the law. He was accused of assaulting two different men in Michigan on two consecutive days. He was also charged with carrying a concealed weapon. He received three years probation for both incidents. That means he had to visit a government probation officer once a month. He also had to go to counseling sessions and undergo alcohol and drug testing. He could have been sentenced to a lengthy term in jail.

But for Eminem, nearly going to jail was a wake-up call; he has proclaimed it "almost a blessing in disguise." Since then he has reportedly given up drugs and drinking. His famous workaholic attitude and perfectionist standards are more intense than ever. "Something really bad could have hap-

a Simpsons-like world, occupied by misfits and ruled mercilessly by an unpredictable king." Eminem acknowledges that, bottom line, he wants to entertain listeners. "Rap, overall, is entertainment," he said. "I'm trying to bring it in an entertaining way that's clever — you never know what's going to come, what I'm going to say next. I try to catch people off guard with punch lines. I catch myself off guard a lot of times when I'm writing."

The Marshall Mathers LP debuted at No. 1 on U.S. album charts and became the fastest-selling rap album ever, eventually selling over eight mil-

pened to me. I could be in jail. I could have been shot. I could have been killed," Eminem said. "And I'm proud of myself now for not only my accomplishments but for pulling through all that."

Since the release of *8 Mile*, Eminem has reached a wider audience. The movie seemed to appeal to many people who wouldn't have normally been interested in the rap star. Director Curtis Hanson said, "So many people have come to me and said, 'I had this impression of Eminem and of hip-hop in general, and this movie completely turned me around.' I couldn't get a better compliment. And neither could Marshall."

While many are still offended by Eminem's lyrics and his content, they are for the most part keeping quiet these days. With his huge album sales—30 million and counting—and his worldwide exposure in *8 Mile*, he seems to have achieved an almost mainstream acceptance. The *New York Times Magazine* put him on their cover labeled "American Idol." The *New York Times* is known as a staid and serious newspaper, but its columnist Maureen Dowd said she had a "yuppie love" for Eminem and called him "as cuddly as Beaver Cleaver." Eminem is distinctly uncomfortable with this turn of events. He responded to the Dowd column: "That's when it's getting bad. That's when it gets scary. When everyone loves you, who's left to hate you? The kids want something they can hold onto that their parents hate." At this point, much of the public condemnation of Eminem seems to have subsided.

lion copies. In addition, it was the first rap record ever to be nominated for the "Album of the Year" category in the Grammy Awards. Although it didn't win, it took home prizes in two other categories. The album won Eminem more fans than ever—but riled more critics, too. When Eminem was invited to perform at the MTV Video Music Awards in September 2000, he was widely denounced. Women's groups and other entertainers denounced him as a terrible influence on young listeners, and the Gay and Lesbian Alliance Against Defamation (GLAAD) staged a protest. A spokesperson from GLAAD said that "These are the words that kids hear in school hall-ways before they get beat up. For this kind of language to be put out there without any sense of responsibility on Eminem's part, or MTV's part, is simply not something that GLAAD can ignore. . . .We are very disappoint-ed that they continue to support him as heavily as they do." The U.S. Senate even heard testimony against him.

> —————— " ——————
>
> *A spokesperson from GLAAD said that "These are the words that kids hear in school hallways before they get beat up. For this kind of language to be put out there without any sense of responsibility on Eminem's part, or MTV's part, is simply not something that GLAAD can ignore. . . .We are very disappointed that they continue to support him as heavily as they do."*
>
> —————— " ——————

As for the anti-gay charges, Eminem has reacted with bewilderment. He said he is not homophobic (someone who hates homosexuals) but het-erophiliac (someone who loves the opposite sex). "If I said in one of my songs ["My Name Is"] that my Eng-lish teacher wanted to have sex with me in junior high, all I'm saying is that, I'm not gay you know?" he said. "People confuse the lyrics for me speaking my mind. I don't agree with that lifestyle, but if that lifestyle is for you, then it's your business." He made an apparent peace offering to the gay community at the Grammy Awards telecast in 2001. Eminem pointedly performed "Stan" with Elton John, the rock star who is openly gay. The two hugged at the end of the performance. (Ever the rebel, Eminem also made an obscene gesture. But that was edited out of the broadcast.) For his own part, Eminem says that his critics misunderstand him. "[At] the end of the day, it's all a joke," he said of his work. "Anybody with a sense of humor is going to put on my album and laugh from beginning to end."

The Eminem Show

During his rocket-ride to fame, Eminem stayed loyal to his old neighbor-hood and friends. He continued to live in the Detroit area. The Bass broth-ers still produced most of his tracks. And he kept working with five long-time friends in a rap crew called D12, or Dirty Dozen. In June 2001, the group released an album, *Devil's Night*. The effort produced a couple of top singles and eventually went to No. 1. It was also notable because it ap-peared on Eminem's own new record label, Shady Records.

But even sticking to familiar people and surroundings, Eminem couldn't sidestep the hassles of his newfound celebrity. His personal problems and run-ins with the law had been trumpeted in the media [see the sidebar entitled "Eminem's Changing Reputation," pages 46–47]. Long-lost friends and family members (including his father) were trying to get a piece of him. "Sometimes I don't know where my private life ends and my public life begins," he said. "It all seems to blend together a lot. I feel like there's nothing that I can do that is not wrote about, at least at this time in my life."

His next major album, *The Eminem Show* (2002), airs his gripes about life as a celebrity, a life that no longer feels like his own. As a reviewer for *Entertainment Weekly* observed, Eminem "plays to a culture obsessed with celebrity gossip and talk-show voyeurism at the same time it rails against that culture." He rants blisteringly about his mother in "Cleanin' Out My Closet." He delves into his divorce in "Superman." Beating his detractors at their own game, as always, he faces the charge that he peddles black music to white masses for his own profit: "I am the worst thing since Elvis Presley, To do black music so selfishly/and use it to get myself wealthy." Elsewhere he acknowledges, "Look at my sales/Let's do the math, If I was black I woulda sold half." His song "White America" scorns two vice presidents' wives, Lynne Cheney and Tipper Gore, and trashes the moral hypocrisy of middle America. He charges his critics with racism: he asserts that critics didn't object to rap music when it appealed to African-American kids, but that critics now complain because his rap music appeals to white kids. "See the problem is I speak to suburban kids who otherwise would of never knew these words exist/ . . . they connected with me too because I looked like them/that's why [critics] put my lyrics up under this microscope, searchin' with a fine tooth comb/ . . . All I hear is: lyrics, lyrics, constant controversy, sponsors working round the clock, to try to stop my concerts early/surely hip-hop was never a problem in Harlem only in Boston, after it bothered the fathers of daughters starting to blossom/so now I'm catchin' the flack from these activists."

But alongside the usual rage and profanity, critics note a softer tone to *The Eminem Show*. In "Sing for the Moment," he asks his critics to consider his tenderness to his daughter. He asks, "It's all political, if my music is literal and I'm a criminal/ How . . . can I raise a little girl? /I couldn't. I wouldn't be fit to." He also makes his singing debut with "Hailie's Song." He croons in a falsetto voice, "My baby girl keeps getting older, I watch her grow with pride/People make jokes 'cause they don't understand me, they just don't see my real side."

49

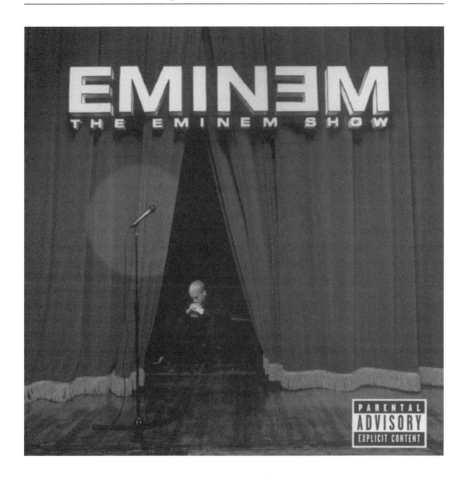

Rolling Stone noted that the song "Without Me" highlights the best and worst of Eminem: "It's his catchiest hit ever, the first one where the music behind him is every bit as extraordinary as his rhymes. . . . His brutal wit, his energy, his inventive rhyme-slinging are all at a peak. So, unfortunately, are the things that people can't stand about Em: his self-pity, his ego, his pomposity, his thin whine, his [cowardly] terror of women and gay people, and everyone else who doesn't fit into his [up-tight] little vision of the world." Several critics shared this general assessment. Eminem's verbal and creative gifts were gleaming as brightly as ever. But wasn't the subject matter wearing a little thin for a maturing artist? Shortly after his 30th birthday, Eminem told Frank Rich of the *New York Times* that he would always have a raw edge to draw on. "But as I grow as a person and as I get older I've got to mature," he said. "If you think that the only way I can make a record is by cussing, then I'll make a different record to outsmart you and prove you wrong."

The Eminem Show was a great success with critics and listeners alike. It won five Grammy nominations, including nominations for the coveted Album of the Year and Record of the Year awards. It eventually won two awards: Best Rap Album and Best Short Form Music Video, for "Without Me." In addition, it has sold over seven million copies.

8 Mile

In November 2002 Eminem surprised fans and critics with his charismatic film debut as a lead actor. In 8 Mile, Eminem plays a fictional version of himself as struggling, would-be Detroit rapper Jimmy "Rabbit" Smith. When we meet him, he has just "choked" on stage at an important rap battle. He stands speechless and miserable while a rowdy crowd jeers him. We learn that his girlfriend has left him carless and homeless. He is forced to live in a beat-up trailer with his luckless mother (played by Kim Basinger) and neglected little sister, whom he adores. To make matters worse, his mom is sleeping with an obnoxious idiot whom Jimmy knew—and hated—in high school.

— " —

"["Without Me"is] his catchiest hit ever, the first one where the music behind him is every bit as extraordinary as his rhymes. . . . His brutal wit, his energy, his inventive rhyme-slinging are all at a peak. So, unfortunately, are the things that people can't stand about Em: his self-pity, his ego, his pomposity, his thin whine, his [cowardly] terror of women and gay people, and everyone else who doesn't fit into his [up-tight] little vision of the world." — **Rolling Stone**

— " —

We follow Jimmy through a week of his life. He works at a dead-end factory job, hangs with his engaging, mostly African-American group of friends, and works doggedly toward the dream of a demo record and rap recognition. Along the way, romantic interest appears in the form of Alex (played by Brittany Murphy). She is an aspiring model who's out for herself, but she believes in his future. The film ends with an electrifying contest of rappers' wits. Though Jimmy triumphs in the battle, he hasn't won the war. We don't know what his future holds. But we get a sense that he has gained a better understanding of his own talent and where it can take him.

Eminem did no more than six weeks' intensive rehearsal as preparation for his lead role in the film, which he called a "grueling" process. But Curtis Hanson, the director of 8 Mile, said Eminem's performance was not a result of rehearsing. "This is a person who loves words, who loves rolling them around on his tongue, like most real actors do," Hanson said. "He's a great improviser, obviously, extremely quick on his feet. And while he can be extremely intense, he's also very funny. But most of all, whatever that magical thing is that draws us to people on the screen, he had it. All I had to do, really, was put a frame around it."

Eminem added to the movie's authenticity with steady input. He and his friends helped the screenwriter nail the language and concerns of their crowd. He provided the title. And Eminem apparently uses the film to answer his critics. It portrays his alter-ego rapper Jimmy as basically hard-working, purposeful, and devoted to his friends and sister. And the first time we see the character Rabbit really let go and rap, it's to defend a gay co-worker who was ridiculed by a rival rapper. Jimmy shoots him down with a clever, rapid-fire spree. "Paul's gay," he spits, "But you're a faggot." The scene demonstrates Eminem's contention that in the rap world, "faggot" can be an all-purpose put down, not an anti-gay slur.

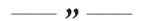

> *When asked whether he wants to be a movie star, Eminem said, "I never intended that. I wanted to make a movie because I felt my story was unique, but at the same time not. If other roles [come up]? I don't know. I'll be too old to rap someday. Or when the music slows down. Then maybe, yeah, I'll take another role."*

The film boasts a top-flight Hollywood director, Curtis Hanson. And its producer, screenwriter, and cinematographer are also A-list talents. Even so, many were suspicious that this was merely a vehicle for exploiting Eminem's stardom, and the film industry was very cautious about the movie's potential. So the film's critical and commercial success were way beyond expectations. Critics praised the realistically gritty Detroit setting and the talented supporting cast. But many acknowledged that the force carrying the show was novice Eminem, who appears in nearly every scene. They responded to the authenticity of the story and to his powerful performance. "Compact, volatile, and burningly intense, he's got charisma to spare," noted David Ansen in *Newsweek*. Richard Schickel said in *Time* magazine that Eminem "understands the power of being still in front of the camera. He's a kid with the ability to put a sullen but seductive face on an open heart." But some critics found his performance too passive and understated. They would have liked to see him harness his famous humor

A scene from the movie 8 Mile. *Jimmy (Eminem) and the Three One Three crew go for a ride in the Motor City. Left to right: Future (Mekhi Phifer), Cheddar Bob (Evan Jones), and DJ LZ (DeAngelo Wilson).*

and anger. "A toned-down Eminem brings nothing special to the screen," said the reviewer for *People* magazine. Still, *8 Mile* proved to be a smash hit with fans. It was No. 1 after its first weekend in theaters, earning $54.5 million at the box office.

Viewers also enjoyed the great music, sending the *8 Mile* movie sound-track to No. 1 on the music charts when it debuted. On the movie sound-track, Eminem performs only five of the album's 16 songs—plus one with D12. In the title track "8 Mile," Eminem fires out 1,100 words in six minutes—and is credited with a masterful performance. The track "Lose Yourself" won acclaim as a great song of the year. In it, Eminem powerfully conveys the hunger for success and the importance of believing in your own talent, against all odds. In March 2003, "Lose Yourself" won an Academy Award for the best song in a film, becoming the first rap song ever to win an Academy Award.

Plans for the Future

Eminem has no immediate plans for future acting jobs. When asked whether he wants to be a movie star, he said, "I never intended that. I wanted to make a movie because I felt my story was unique, but at the same time not. If other roles [come up]? I don't know. I'll be too old to rap someday. Or when the music slows down. Then maybe, yeah, I'll take another role."

Since meeting Dr. Dre, Eminem has become more and more involved with producing music. He even helped Dr. Dre produce his own Chronic album, at Dr. Dre's request. With the launch of his label, Shady Records, producing consumes more of Eminem's time and interest. As of early 2003, he was producing his old crew D12, as well as acts like ObieTrice and 50 Cent, a New York rapper expected to hit it big. "I'm trying to build my clientele," he said, foreseeing a career one day as a record-label head and producer. "Eventually I want to branch off into being a producer and be able to one day sit back like Dre and kind of be behind the scenes and not always have to be the front man," he said.

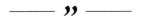

"*[Every] song that I make has to be better than the last one that I just made. Otherwise it gets scrapped. Because if you're not doing that, you're stagnant.*"

As for his own music, Eminem wants to keep growing. "[Every] song that I make has to be better than the last one that I just made," he said. "Otherwise it gets scrapped. Because if you're not doing that, you're stagnant."

MARRIAGE AND FAMILY

Eminem has called his longtime partner Kimberly Ann Scott "the first true girlfriend I ever had." The couple has been romantically linked since they were young teenagers — and have apparently spent the subsequent years breaking up and making up. They met when Eminem's mother took in the 12-year-old Kim. Eminem and Kim became romantically involved in the 1980s, had a daughter, Hailie Jade, in December 1995, and were married in June 1999. "Me and the missus, we go at it. It's no secret that we've had our problems," Eminem said. "Once you bring a child into this world, it makes it that much more complicated, especially when you don't get along with someone. You're trying to make it work, you want to make your family work, but [stuff] keeps happening that [screws] it up."

Their stormy relationship has inspired several notorious songs, including "97 Bonnie and Clyde" and "Kim," both violent revenge fantasies. "Kim has been the basis of a lot of his songs," said Eminem's longtime friend Jay Fields. "Pain, mystery, and drama — that's what motivates an artist, as much as love and affection." In July 2000, Kim Mathers attempted suicide while Eminem was performing at a nearby arena. A month later she sued him for "intentional infliction of emotional distress" for the lyrics of "Kim." She also threatened to deny him access to Hailie. They reached a settlement with an undisclosed cash award. They then attempted to reconcile. But it didn't work, and they divorced in 2001. Kim Mathers got physical custody of Hailie, while Eminem won legal custody and visitation rights.

Eminem acknowledged that his unexpected success and fame has been tough for the couple to handle. "Not to defend Kim, but I realize what has happened with me has probably been a strain on her too," Eminem said. "It's a crazy thing to deal with. You've really got to be in shape." After his divorce, Eminem was romantically linked for a short time with the singer Mariah Carey. There were also rumors that he was involved with his *8 Mile* co-stars, Brittany Murphy and Kim Basinger. There have also been media reports that he and his ex-wife have reunited.

If Eminem's relationship with his ex-wife has its ups and downs, his dealings with his mother are mostly down. Amid much publicity, Deborah Nelson sued her son in September 1999 for $10 million. She claimed that Eminem slandered her in press and radio interviews by suggesting that she was unstable and a drug user. A year later she filed another suit for $1 million. In total, she received settlements of $25,000. Eminem apparently doesn't communicate with her.

Amid his domestic problems, Eminem takes great joy in his relationship with his daughter. "I'm a father before anything," he said. A longtime friend called Eminem a big kid who loves to make his daughter laugh. He is said to do a great Kermit the Frog imitation. "He's a good daddy," the friend said. "He's trying to give Hailie more of a normal life than he had." They live in a large brown brick house in a gated neighborhood in the affluent northern suburbs of Detroit — much closer to 26 Mile Road than to 8 Mile Road. Eminem likes to feed Hailie breakfast and take her to school. She enjoys visiting him in the studio and has contributed to tracks on his records. When they play his music in the car, Eminem turns down the volume on the swear words. And cussing isn't allowed in front of Hailie. "She has a fairly normal life," Eminem said. "I love her so much."

RECORDINGS

Infinite, 1997
The Slim Shady EP, 1997
The Slim Shady LP, 1998
Just Don't Give a F——, 1998

The Marshall Mathers LP, 2000
Devil's Night, 2001 (with D12)
8 Mile: The Soundtrack, 2002
The Eminem Show, 2002

FILMS

8 Mile, 2002

BOOKS

Eminem: Angry Blonde, 2000

HONORS AND AWARDS

MTV Music Video Awards: 1999, for Best New Artist Award; 2000 (three
    awards), for Video of the Year, Best Male Video, and Best Rap Video, for
    "Forgot About Dre"; 2002 (four awards), for Video of the Year, Best Male
    Video, Best Rap Video, and Best Direction, all for "Without Me"
Grammy Awards: 2000 (two awards), Best Rap Album, for *The Slim Shady
    LP*, Best Rap Solo Performance, for "My Name Is"; 2001 (three awards),
    Best Rap Album, for *The Marshall Mathers LP*, Best Rap Solo
    Performance, for "The Real Slim Shady," Best Rap Performance by a Duo
    or Group, for "Forget about Dre" (with Dr. Dre); 2003 (two awards), for
    Best Rap Album, for *The Eminem Show*, Best Short Form Music Video, for
    "Without Me"
Billboard Music Awards: 2000 (two awards), for Maximum Vision Video
    and Best Rap/Hip-Hop Clip of the Year, for "The Real Slim Shady; 2002
    (two awards), Album of the Year and R&B/Hip-Hop Album of the Year,
    both for *The Eminem Show*
Europe Music Awards: 2002 (three awards), for Best Male Artist, Best Hip-
    Hop Artist, and Best Album, all for *The Eminem Show*
American Music Awards: 2003 (four awards), Best Pop-Rock Male Artist,
    Best Soul/Rhythm & Blues Male Artist, Best Soul/Rhythm & Blues
    Album, and Best Pop-Rock Album, all for *The Eminem Show*
People's Choice Award: 2003, for Favorite Male Musical Performer
Academy Award (Oscar): 2003, for Best Song, for "Lose Yourself"

FURTHER READING

Books

Contemporary Musicians, Vol. 28, 2000
Eminem: Angry Blonde, 2000

Periodicals

Current Biography Yearbook, 2001
Detroit Free Press, Feb. 28, 1999, p.E1
Detroit News, Nov. 8, 2002, p.1
Entertainment Weekly, Nov. 8, 2002, p.20
Los Angeles Times, Feb. 7, 1999, p.3
New York Times, Nov. 17, 2002, p.L12
New York Times Magazine, Nov. 3, 2002, p.52
New Yorker, Nov. 11, 2002
Newsweek, May 29, 2000, p.62
People, Dec. 25, 2000, p. 64; July 24, 2000, p.139; July 8, 2002, p.111
Rolling Stone, May 23, 2002, p.23; July 4, 2002, pp.70 and 107
Teen, Feb. 2001, p.40
Teen People, May 15, 2001, p.34; Oct. 1, 2002, pp.104 and 110
Time, May 29, 2000, p. 73; Nov. 11, 2002, p.85
Vibe, Nov. 2002, p.91
Washington Post, July 27, 1999, p.C1

Online Database

Biography Resource Center Online, 2003, article from *Contemporary Musicians*, 2000

ADDRESS

Eminem
Interscope Records
10900 Wilshire Boulevard
Suite 1230
Los Angeles, CA 90024

WORLD WIDE WEB SITES

http://www.eminem.com
http://www.mtv.com/bands/az/eminem/artist.jhtml
http://www.rollingstone.com/artists/default.asp?oid=6395
http://www.vh1.com/artists/az/eminem/artist.jhtml

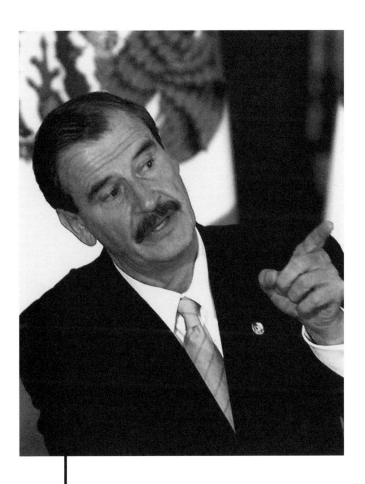

Vicente Fox 1942-
Mexican Political and Business Leader
President of Mexico

BIRTH

Vicente Fox was born Vicente Fox Quesada in Mexico City, Mexico, on July 2, 1942. In Mexico and other Spanish-speaking cultures, it is common for a child to be given the last name of both the father and the mother, the first being the father's and the second being the mother's. Vicente Fox's father, Jose Luis Fox, was a rancher in the Mexican state of Guanajuato who was born in Mexico. He was the son of an Irish immigrant who had first lived in Cincinnati, Ohio, and settled in

Mexico in 1913. Fox's mother, Mercedes Quesada, was born in Spain and moved to Mexico with her parents when she was still an infant. Vicente Fox is the second of nine children, with eight sisters and brothers.

YOUTH

Fox grew up on the family ranch in San Francisco del Rincon in the state of Guanajuato, Mexico. The ranch was large, 1,100 acres, and the family grew vegetables and raised animals. They also had family businesses in vegetable canning and boot manufacturing. Most Mexican families are poor, and very few families hold large pieces of property. So in that regard, Fox was born into a privileged family. But in his 1999 autobiography, *Vicente Fox a Los Pinos* (in Spanish), Fox said that he had close ties to poorer children as he grew up. "Something I'm proud of is that I became good friends with the children of the smallholders [owners of smaller farms] and peasants. With them I shared my infancy, my playthings, my house, and my food," he wrote. "From that time I began to understand our country's painful inequalities."

Not a lot has been written about Fox's life as a child. He often refers to his strong Catholic upbringing. His mother said he was an energetic,

> "Something I'm proud of is that I became good friends with the children of the smallholders [owners of smaller farms] and peasants. With them I shared my infancy, my playthings, my house, and my food. From that time I began to understand our country's painful inequalities."

smart, and stubborn boy who would challenge friends to see who could withstand the most bee stings—and he would win. Fox has said that his interest in history and politics took form when he was a young man. One period in history that particularly fascinated him was the time of the Cristeros, who were militant Catholics who launched a rebellion shortly after the Mexican Revolution in 1910. The Cristeros fought the revolutionary government for three years before surrendering. In fact, in later years, as a campaigning politician, he would quote a Cristero battle cry: "If I advance, follow me! If I stop, push me! If I retreat, shoot me!"

For a time, Fox was interested in becoming a bullfighter, but his parents encouraged him to study business instead. His father once warned him about pursuing either farming or politics as a career. "My father only ever gave me two pieces of advice," Fox said. "Study anything but agriculture because a farmer's life is too hard. And, please don't ever get into politics. It's dirty, it's rotten, it's corrupt." Fox joked, "So, I'm a politician and a farmer. I'm a very obedient son."

EDUCATION

Fox attended a Jesuit high school, which is a private, Catholic school run by an order of priests known for valuing knowledge and education. Part of his education included a year at a Jesuit high school in Prairie du Chien, Wisconsin, in the United States. Fellow students described him as a quiet student who did not fit in well.

Fox attended the Universidad Iberoamericana in Mexico City, which was a Jesuit college. He describes himself as a lackadaisical student, and has admitted to trying to cheat on exams. "I distinguished myself only because I was the only one who wore denims [blue jeans] while the great majority wore suits," he wrote in his autobiography. "I sat in the back of the classroom with my body slouched back and my feet stretched out."

Fox left the Universidad Iberoamericana without graduating in 1964, during what would have been his final semester. He later was awarded a degree, by Mexican President Ernesto Zedillo, in 1999.

CAREER HIGHLIGHTS

Climbing the Corporate Ladder

Fox decided to leave school in order to pursue a career opportunity with the Coca Cola Company. His work brought him a lot of business experience, and also expanded his knowledge of the Mexican people, especially in rural areas.

Fox started out as a route salesman. From there, he moved up to a position as route supervisor and eventually became marketing director for all of Coca Cola's Mexican business. He credits his time rising through the ranks at Coca Cola as the foundation of his later success. "At the university, they taught me to reflect and to analyze," he said. "But working at Coca Cola was my second university education. I learned that the heart of a business is out in the field, not in the office. I learned strategy, marketing, financial management, optimization of resources." But perhaps even more important, Fox said, "I learned not to accept anything but winning. I learned an iron discipline for getting results."

Fox's career gave him a close-up view of the Mexican government as well. He has spoken of his biggest frustration being bureaucracy — government that is slowed down by rigid rules and inefficiency. "What I hated most about those years at Coca Cola was the time I had to spend dithering with the government," Fox said. He mentions meetings at *Los Pinos* or "The Pines," the presidential residence in Mexico City, similar to the White House in the United States. The Mexican president would summon important business leaders there, including Fox, "so we could listen to a lot of foolishness."

While Fox was the marketing director for Coca Cola in Mexico, the soft drink passed Pepsi in sales, which had been No. 1 in the market for years. In 1979, Coca Cola offered Fox the opportunity to become the director of all its Latin American operations. Taking the position would have meant relocating to Miami, Florida, or Atlanta, Georgia, and leaving Mexico.

Running the Family Business

While the career move with Coca Cola might have offered Fox both prestige and money, he decided that living in Mexico was more important. After 15 years of success with the company, Fox resigned and moved back home to Guanajuato to work with his brothers in the family's business.

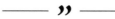

"At the university, they taught me to reflect and to analyze. But working at Coca Cola was my second university education. I learned that the heart of a business is out in the field, not in the office. I learned strategy, marketing, financial management, optimization of resources." But perhaps even more important, Fox said, "I learned not to accept anything but winning. I learned an iron discipline for getting results."

The family business, Grupo Fox, included primarily vegetable growing and boot and shoe manufacturing. The business grew as Fox added his marketing experience to the family's efforts. The 1980s brought a lot of difficulty to small- and medium-sized businesses in Mexico, however. The Mexican currency, the peso, went through a series of devaluations, and inflation was high. Because of the ability to sell their boots and shoes in markets other than Mexico, Grupo Fox stayed in business while many other businesses failed. "Every micro, small, and medium-sized entrepreneur in this country is a hero for surviving, growing, and exporting under these circumstances," Fox said of that period in Mexico's economic history.

Fox rides a horse on his ranch in San Cristobal, June 2000.

Entering the Political Arena

In the late 1980s, Fox's business dealings brought him into increasing contact with the government—and reinforced his belief in the need for change. At the time a close friend, Manuel Clouthier, was running for president. Clouthier encouraged Fox to consider politics as a career change. He persuaded Fox to join the National Action Party (PAN), which opposed the Institutional Republican Party (PRI), the party that had dominated Mexican politics for more than 70 years. [For an explanation of the PRI and PAN, see the sidebar on "Mexico: Power and Turmoil," pages 65–67.]

In 1988, Fox ran for Congress on the PAN ticket and won by a three-to-one margin. Part of his success in the election campaign was due to establishing his own fund-raising organization, called Friends of Fox. In this shrewd and forward-thinking move, he both distanced himself from the influence of PAN leadership and created a vehicle for funding future campaigns should he ever lose the support of PAN.

Making Waves

Fox immediately drew attention to himself in the Mexican Congress. In the same election year, 1988, PRI candidate Carlos Salinas was elected president in what many considered to be fraudulent circumstances. The race with the PRD candidate, Cuauhtemoc Cardenas, had been close; in fact, early returns indicated that Cardenas was in the lead. But PRI-controlled election officials suddenly announced that computers tabulating the election returns had crashed due to "atmospheric conditions." When the counting resumed, Salinas had taken the lead.

When the Mexican Congress met to confirm the election of Salinas, Fox ascended the podium with two charred ballots taped to the side of his head, representing Salinas's large ears. In a voice that mimicked Salinas, Fox said, "I've felt obligated to ask many of my friends to set aside moral scruples to help me achieve this victory, which I had to do because Mexico isn't ready for democracy." He summed up the comic satire of the president-elect by saying, "The truth is that the people did not vote for me; my friends had to stuff the ballot boxes."

Fox has created a political style that is open, brash, and very easy to understand by the average Mexican citizen. Throughout his political career, he's sported the *vaquero*—or cowboy—look of his native state of Guanajuato. Even in the legislative assembly, he'd sometimes wear jeans, cowboy boots, and an open shirt instead of the traditional suit and tie. His striking good looks and tall stature have also made him stand out from many of his counterparts.

And unlike other politicians, Fox has often used common Mexican slang in his speech-making, even to the point of occasionally using profanity. This common touch has served him well in his political career.

Battling the PRI

After serving two years in the Mexican legislature, Fox returned to Guanajuato to run for governor in the state's 1991 election. Hugely popular among Guanajuato's citizens and openly critical of the PRI and President Salinas, Fox invited the wrath of the PRI and all its resources. First, Salinas tried to dilute Fox's candidacy by reversing a court decision that would have prevented a second opposition candidate—in effect, taking support away from Fox.

Then, on election day, more votes were counted than there were registered voters, suggesting either ballot stuffing or manipulation of the numbers. The PRI candidate, of course, had "defeated" Fox. The PRI-controlled electoral commission certified that the ballots were correctly tabulated. But Fox publicly challenged the election results, backed by an angry group of thousands of supporters. Pressured by public opinion, the PRI admitted to the miscount. Instead of pronouncing either Fox or the PRI candidate the winner, they installed a PAN candidate in the governorship who was not even on the ballot.

After Fox failed in his bid for the governorship, however, key changes began to take place in the federal government that would eventually pave the way for his presidential election. President Salinas and his regime had been exposed for corruption and mismanagement of the economy. And there were indications of serious wrongdoing at the highest level. A number of key politicians had disappeared or been assassinated during the Salinas presidency. President Salinas's brother had been arrested and later found guilty of conspiracy to commit murder of a prominent PRI official. Salinas left office in 1994. The country was in an economic shambles, and public trust of the federal government was shaken. In the wake of his brother's arrest, Salinas left the country with millions of dollars in 1995.

Fox had long made clear his intention to run for Mexico's presidential office, even back in 1991 when running for governor. A law in the Mexican constitution, however, prevented him from running. The law stated that both of a candidate's parents had to have been born in Mexico; Fox's mother had been born in Spain. In 1993, the PRI-controlled legislature was publicly pressured to change the law. But they prevented Fox from running for president in 1994 by writing a provision that the new law would not take effect until the year 2000.

The new president in 1994 was Ernesto Zedillo. Despite his PRI affiliation, Zedillo instituted many reforms in Mexico's federal government [see the sidebar on "Mexico: Power and Turmoil," pages 65-67]. Most importantly, he established an independent electoral commission to oversee elections, despite the objection of his party.

Governor Fox

By 1995, when Fox made another run at becoming Guanajuato's governor, the political climate had changed enough that fair elections would be ensured. In a staggering victory, Fox beat his opponent by a two-to-one margin. This was the most dramatic win by an opposition candidate in a gubernatorial election in Mexico's history.

Fox made it his mission while governor of Guanajuato to improve the economic well-being of the state. He relied on his varied experience as a businessman — both as an executive in the large corporate enterprise of Coca Cola and as a director of a family business. With this experience, Fox saw commerce as the way to improve the lives of the people.

Fox traveled constantly, both within the state of Guanajuato and also to the United States and other Latin American countries. Throughout his travels, he sought further business development and opportunity for the state. Under his direction and leadership, Guanajuato became the fifth wealthiest state in Mexico.

One of Fox's concerns was the migration of Mexican labor to the United States. Laborers could earn $60 a day in the United States, instead of an

Mexico: Power and Turmoil

For centuries, Mexico has seen one power struggle after another. In pre-Columbian times (before Columbus came to the New World), Mexico was inhabited by highly advanced cultures. The Olmecs, Mayans, and Aztecs were civilizations that had complex governmental systems, large-scale war, slavery, and taxes. In contrast to the natives of what is now the United States, the indigenous Mexicans had huge cities and large population centers.

The Spanish conquistadors (conquerors and explorers) led by Hernando Cortes landed in Mexico in 1519. The Spanish colonized and enslaved the native peoples, and power shifted from the war-like Aztecs to the militarily superior Europeans. In addition, conquistadors crushed the native religions, which often involved ritual human sacrifice, and people were forced to convert to Catholicism.

Three hundred years of oppression by the Spanish throne came to a close in 1810, when Mexico declared its independence. Eleven years of bloody fighting followed before Spain recognized Mexico's sovereignty. A number of governments followed in the next ninety years, some of them resembling Old World monarchy, some of them mimicking the United States, at least in the name of the office of president. During this time, California, Texas, New Mexico, and Arizona, which had been part of Mexico, became part of the United States, resulting in war and the loss of resources.

The Mexican Revolution, which was a violent and bloody uprising, began in 1910. Pancho Villa and Emiliano Zapata became folk heroes because of the armed bands they led, and some of their Robin Hood-like escapades. The Mexican Revolution sought three goals: to reduce the power of the Catholic church; to remove land from the hands of a few and distribute it to the people; and to take control of precious natural resources (gold, silver, and oil) from foreign interests.

In 1917 a new constitution was created. It signaled the beginning of a federal democratic system that loosely resembled that of the United States. The new government established 31 states (the actual official name of Mexico is *Los Estados Unidos de Mexico*, or the United States of Mexico) and a federal district. A representative congress was formed, and regular elections were established. The executive office of president was created to allow for one term only, with no opportunity for re-election.

The group of revolutionaries who drafted the new constitution became the Institutional Revolutionary Party, which is *Partido Revolucionaria Institucional* in Spanish, known as PRI. This party represented a seat of power that dominated the Mexican government for the next 71 years.

Technically and legally speaking, Mexico was a democracy with its citizens free to create competing political parties. But in reality, it was very difficult to ensure fair election practices. The PRI has been compared with earlier oppressive regimes in the country and has been charged with corruption, deception, censorship of the press, fraud, and theft. And in more recent

average $5 a day in Mexico. This difference has prompted many Mexicans, especially young men, to leave their country to work in the U.S. and send money home. Fox instituted a program to persuade Mexican workers abroad to send 25% of their earnings to be put into what he called "productive investment," like shops or factories, instead of just consumption (living expenses). And the state would match whatever funds were accumulated. This program resulted in 35 new enterprises, creating jobs that made it possible for workers to stay home and work instead of leaving the country.

years, the PRI has been implicated in the killings and disappearance of individuals who opposed their control of the country.

The PRI has held an iron grip on many social institutions, including government, business, and labor. Still, other major parties have slowly emerged. The two most important are the National Action Party, which is *Partido Acción Nacional* in Spanish, known as PAN, and the Party of the Democratic Revolution, which is *Partido Revolucionaria Democratica*, known as PRD. Opposing the PRI, however, was dangerous at times and often unfruitful, as the PRI controlled the whole election process, including the counting of ballots and voter registration.

In the 1980s and 1990s, however, democracy began to make some gains. In the 1994 presidential elections a record 78% of registered voters cast ballots. Ernesto Zedillo of the PRI won with 49% of the votes. The PAN candidate won 26% and the PRD candidate won 17% of the votes. Also, many congressmen and governors were elected from the opposition parties. The PRI was beginning to lose power.

During Zedillo's presidency, massive election reforms took place, including the establishment of an electoral college and equal public funding of political campaigns. These reforms resulted in an electoral process not unlike that of the United States. In fact, in the presidential election of 2000, one of the people entrusted with observing a fair election was former U.S. President Jimmy Carter. That process resulted in the election of PAN candidate Vicente Fox to the presidency.

With the election of President Fox, many Mexicans and foreign observers see the realization of democracy and the opportunity for Mexican citizens to have greater control of their government.

The Road to *"Los Pinos"*

Though intently focused on improving the state of Guanajuato, Fox's sights were set on the Mexican presidency. He made his intentions for the 2000 race public while he was still governor. He announced his candidacy in mid-1997, giving him a full two-and-a-half years to campaign and defeat the PRI.

Fox campaigned aggressively, traveling across Mexico and meeting with people at all levels of society. His working man's appearance and straight

President Vicente Fox, accompanied by his daughter, Paulina, and his son, Rodrigo, wave to the crowd en route to the National Palace following his inauguration ceremony, December 2000.

talk got the attention of poor people, while his business experience and his ideas for economic development attracted middle- and upper-class people. Fox's popularity grew as people became more aware of what kind of person he was.

Fox's political style was aptly described by journalist Dick Reavis, writing for *Texas Monthly*: "The Mexican masses noted Fox's pigstickers [cowboy boots] and rodeo-style belt buckles when they saw him on TV, and they chuckled when they heard him give voice to words from their own blue vernacular. The few of them who read newspapers or tuned into pundits found nothing in the rest of him but confirmation of what those symbols plainly said: that Vicente Fox was a president who would speak from the heart of the common man. Against this message, the PRI was nearly powerless."

Electoral reforms instituted by then-President Zedillo made funds available for television advertising for the first time to a non-PRI candidate. This helped Fox immensely, and he hired people to "sell" him in the same way that advertisers would sell any product. Fox campaigned on promises to end corruption in the government, improve economic growth, and focus on building the educational system in Mexico. And for the first time in Mexican history, the elections would be administered by an independent group of observers—not controlled by the PRI.

On Election Day 2000, the confidence of the people was high, resulting in 64% of Mexico's registered voters casting ballots. The PRI opposition was strong, but its influence was not strong enough to impede what many regard as the first fair election in Mexican history. On July 2, 2000, Fox defeated PRI candidate Francisco Labastida and PRD candidate Cuahtemoc Cardenas, who was Mexico City's mayor. Fox won with more than 43% of the vote. He was the first non-PRI president to occupy the presidential residence, *Los Pinos*, since the Mexican Revolution more than 70 years earlier.

—— **"** ——

"The Mexican masses noted Fox's pigstickers [cowboy boots] and rodeo-style belt buckles when they saw him on TV, and they chuckled when they heard him give voice to words from their own blue vernacular. The few of them who read newspapers or tuned into pundits found nothing in the rest of him but confirmation of what those symbols plainly said: that Vicente Fox was a president who would speak from the heart of the common man. Against this message, the PRI was nearly powerless." —Dick Reavis, **Texas Monthly**

—— **"** ——

The Challenge of Keeping Promises

On President Fox's inauguration day, he spent the morning having breakfast with street children in Mexico City's toughest neighborhood, Tepito. It was his way of saying he would not forget Mexico's poor or the tradition of crime and conflict that have been such a large part of Mexico's history.

"My commitment will be to move Mexico from a path of corruption and impunity, from a path where no one pays attention to education and human capital, and move on to a path of high-speed growth, with a state of law and with an educational revolution," Fox stated early in his presidency. Even after being elected, Fox offered promises of more jobs, better education, and more opportunity for growth.

But being the country's first president who wasn't supported by the PRI, Fox did not have the power base to effect change easily. Much of the legislature and the federal government was made up of PRI supporters. His desire to reform and to eliminate corruption met with opposition in many cases.

Other circumstances that have nothing to do with Mexico's political make-up have prevented noticeable progress. A week before the terrorist attacks on the United States on September 11, 2001, Fox was in Washington, D.C., proposing increased cooperation between the United States and Mexico. He has made no secret of his belief that the U.S. and Mexican economy are closely linked. In his visit with President Bush on September 8, 2001, Fox proposed more lenient immigration standards for Mexicans. Fox hoped that through more open immigration policy, money from émigrés to the United States would fuel economic growth back home. The theory is that products, labor, and money would flow more freely across the border, benefitting both countries.

> "My commitment will be to move Mexico from a path of corruption and impunity, from a path where no one pays attention to education and human capital, and move on to a path of high-speed growth, with a state of law and with an educational revolution," Fox stated early in his presidency.

But with the attacks on September 11, the Bush administration quickly became focused on combating terrorism and addressing the faltering economy in the United States. Mexico and other countries have also shared the economic slump that has affected the United States. While Fox had promised to create 1.5 million jobs during his administration, he had to admit that more than 200,000 jobs had been lost during his first year in office.

Battling Corruption and Criticism

Fox has also been the object of criticism in his pledge to fight corruption in Mexico, particularly in the area of human rights. Early in his administration, key drug lords were arrested who had formerly been protected by corrupt law enforcement. These arrests earned him high praise. He made an open agenda of battling *la impunidad* (Spanish for "the impunity," or lack of consequences for wrongdoing among government officials and police). He initiated new access to government files on incidents that had

President Vicente Fox and his wife Martha Sahagun attend a state dinner at the White House with President George W. Bush and First Lady Laura Bush, September 2001.

been questionable in the past. Most notable was the opening of a long-secret file on the 1968 massacre of hundreds of protesting students.

Despite these early actions, many have voiced concern that Fox was not doing enough to reform the corrupt system that had been in place for years. This criticism increased with the assassination in October 2001 of Digna Ochoa, a key human rights leader. Ochoa was a human rights attorney who gained popularity by representing people who accused the police and military of kidnaping, torture, and murder. A note found at the scene of her murder made it clear that she was killed for her human rights work.

Opponents of Fox have claimed that he has not done enough to solve Ochoa's murder. Fox did, however, initiate a commission to investigate the disappearances and deaths of more than 500 anti-government activists since the late 1970s. For the first time in Mexican history, an official report admitted government involvement in some of the cases.

Despite such criticism, Fox remains committed to change for Mexico. In an address in June 2002 that marked the one-year anniversary of his inauguration, Fox said, "Friends, I am a man of my word and I know how to keep my word—this is what I learned from my parents, and I will try to keep my word to all of you. All the promises made during my campaign are being met. One year has not been much time to achieve the great objectives I proposed during the campaign. However, it has been more than enough time to show clearly that we are ready to guarantee the enormous changes that we wanted for our country, for our people, for our families, for our daughters and sons.... The future is ours."

> "Friends, I am a man of my word and I know how to keep my word—this is what I learned from my parents, and I will try to keep my word to all of you. All the promises made during my campaign are being met. One year has not been much time to achieve the great objectives I proposed during the campaign. However, it has been more than enough time to show clearly that we are ready to guarantee the enormous changes that we wanted for our country, for our people, for our families, for our daughters and sons.... The future is ours."

Fox has set an ambitious series of goals for his presidency, and whether he will be able to achieve all these goals in his six-year term remains to be seen. He will, however, be regarded in Mexican history as the leader who successfully broke the rule of the PRI and challenged the corrupt systems that have plagued Mexico for centuries.

MARRIAGE AND FAMILY

In 1971, Fox married Lillian de la Concha, who worked as a secretary at Coca Cola at the time they met. They adopted four children, two daughters (Ana Cristina and Pauline) and two sons (Vicente and Rodrigo). The couple divorced in 1991, and Fox has retained custody of the four children.

During Fox's campaign for the presidency, he became close with his spokesperson, Martha Sahagun. After he was elected, he named her press secretary. One morning, about a year after he was elected, Sahagun was in his office, taking notes on scheduled tasks. "July 2, 8 a.m.," Fox said. "Okay," Sahagun replied, as she noted the date. "What do you want me to do then?" "Marry me," was Fox's reply. July 2 would be a special day: it was the one-year anniversary of Fox's election, and also his birthday.

Fox's remarriage caused some criticism, especially from devoted Catholics. Church custom dictates that if a person hopes to marry a second time, their first marriage should be officially annulled (the church saying in effect that the marriage never existed). Both Fox and Sahagun were divorced, and neither had sought annulments. This caused scandal among some, and signaled to others liberalization from repressive religion. The two were married at *Los Pinos* in a civil ceremony on July 2, 2001.

Vicente Fox and Martha Sahagun smile as they pose during a private wedding ceremony at the presidential residence, Los Pinos, July 2001.

HONORS AND AWARDS

Civic Man of the Year (Alianza Civica — Civic Alliance): 1991
Man of the Year (*Latin Finance*): 2001

FURTHER READING

Books

Contemporary Hispanic Biography, Vol. 1, 2002
Encyclopedia of World Biography Supplement, Vol. 21, 2001
Fox, Vicente. *Vicente Fox a Los Pinos,* 1999 (in Spanish)
Paprocki, Sherry Beck, *Vicente Fox (Major World Leaders),* 2003
Who's Who in America, 2002

Periodicals

Atlanta Journal-Constitution, Nov. 11, 2001, p.A5
Current Biography Yearbook, 2001
Hispanic Magazine, May 2001
Newsweek, Nov. 26, 2001, p.66
Texas Monthly, Dec. 2000, p.126

Time, Oct. 15, 2001, p.80
Washington Post, Sep. 4, 2001, p.C1

Online Resources

Biography Resource Center Online, 2003, articles from *Contemporary Hispanic Biography*, 2002, and *Encyclopedia of World Biography Supplement*, 2001

ADDRESS

Presidente Vicente Fox
Los Pinos, México, D.F.
Mexico

WORLD WIDE WEB SITE

http://www.vicentefox.org.mx

Millard Fuller 1935-

American Attorney, Business Leader, and
Philanthropist
Founder of Habitat for Humanity International

BIRTH

Millard Dean Fuller was born on January 3, 1935, in Lanett,
Alabama. He is the son of Render Alexander Fuller, a grocery
store owner, and Estin Cook Fuller. Fuller's mother died when
he was only three. His father later remarried, and his new stepmother was Eunice Stephens Fuller. Fuller has two younger
half-brothers, James Doyle and Render Nicholas, who are the
sons of Fuller's stepmother.

YOUTH

From a very early age Millard Fuller had the makings of a successful businessman—he was an entrepreneur at heart, and he drew his strength to be independent from his family. Although his mother died when he was only three, he grew up in a loving, supportive, and religious family. His father remarried when Fuller was six, and he soon had two half-brothers. Their home community in Sumter County, Alabama, was very poor, and the Fullers struggled as much as anyone there. Fuller's grandfather had been a sharecropper (someone who farms a piece of land owned by someone else), and the family never had a permanent home. "We were always shifting around," Fuller remembered. "That's why I think interest in housing is so deep in my psyche."

> "Since I was a boy, I was involved in several business enterprises. When I was six years old, my father bought me a pig and set me up a bookkeeping system where I could keep track of the expenses and income and profit when I sold the pig. My father was my mentor and inspiration for business. I sold chickens, rabbits, firecrackers, and a few used automobiles. At 19 I was the nation's youngest program director of Junior Achievement in Opelika, Alabama."

Fuller's father worked hard to support his family, and his work ethic rubbed off on his son. "My father ran a grocery store and a soft ice cream shop on the edge of Lanett," Fuller recalled of his childhood years. "I worked there and flipped thousands of hamburgers and made thousands of milkshakes. He later was a cattle farmer, and I helped him sell cattle. I worked planting the fields, harvesting the grain, and baling the hay."

But the young boy did more than help his father; he also ran many of his own business ventures. "Since I was a boy," he said, "I was involved in several business enterprises. When I was six years old, my father bought me a pig and set me up a bookkeeping system where I could keep track of the expenses and income and profit when I sold the pig. My father was my mentor and inspiration for business. I sold chickens, rabbits, firecrackers, and a few used automobiles. At 19 I was the nation's youngest program director of Junior Achievement in Opelika, Alabama." Fuller also started his own worm farm, selling his product as bait for fishermen.

By the time he was 10 years old, Fuller had also gained his first experience in construction. His father had bought 400 acres of land, and there was a small, tumbledown house on it that he helped his father remodel. Little did he know at the time that this early job in construction would serve him so well in running Habitat for Humanity.

EDUCATION

Fuller continued to rely on his business acumen to earn money during his high school and college years. While in high school, he studied, worked on the family farm, was president of the Southeast Conference of Congregational Christian Churches (which later became the United Church of Christ), and raised and sold cattle for money that he saved for college. In 1953 he was accepted for admission at Auburn University, in Auburn, Alabama, where he studied economics and graduated with a B.S. degree in 1957. After receiving his bachelor's degree, Fuller decided he wanted to become a lawyer. He therefore enrolled at the University of Alabama's School of Law. In addition to his studies there, he wrote for the student newspaper and campaigned, unsuccessfully, for student body president. It was there, too, that he met his similarly ambitious friend and business partner, Morris S. Dees, Jr.

Together, Fuller and Dees launched a direct marketing business while they were still in law school, selling anything that seemed to have a customer demand, including holiday wreaths, doormats, bookends, lamps, and even a student directory. They delivered birthday cakes under the company name Bama Cake Service, and they also invested in real estate. Buying a number of rundown houses near the university, Fuller gained more construction experience renovating these homes, which he and Dees would then rent out. "We had a burning desire to be fabulously rich," he said, adding that "we were making $50,000 a year by the time we graduated from law school."

In 1960, Fuller received his law degree; also that year, he served briefly in the U.S. Army as a lieutenant. As he related, he and Dees then went down to Montgomery, Alabama, and opened up a law office. Again, the point of practicing law was to "make money: get the cases that would produce the most money. No interest in how we could right some wrong."

FIRST JOBS

The first few years of Fuller's career after college were marked by the relentless pursuit of wealth. With his law office partner, he also founded the

Fuller working on a house for Habitat for Humanity.

Fuller and Dees Marketing Group in 1960. Both Fuller and Dees were marketing wizards. Just like when they were in school, they sold whatever they could find a demand for, including tractors, tractor cushions, and cookbooks. In fact, their cookbooks did so well that they launched a smaller company called Favorite Recipes Press, publishing such popular works as *Favorite Recipes of American Home Economics Teachers.* "We sold them by the millions," stated Fuller. "But all of that was for one purpose: making a lot of money."

By the age of 29, everything seemed to be going great for Fuller. He was married with children, and he was already a millionaire. "It was a very quick success track," he remarked. "We made a lot of money and got everything that money gets for you: a Lincoln Continental, a cabin on the lake, two speedboats, 2,000 acres of land, 25 horses, hundreds of head of cattle, maids. We were living a fast and very successful life in terms of worldly standards. But the price you pay for that is that something has to give."

CHOOSING A CAREER

What started to give in Fuller's life was his family life, and it was this difficult time that caused him to change his career goals. His wife, Linda, was miserable, because her husband worked so hard that she and the kids never saw him. Even when Fuller came home to dinner, he was often with Dees, and the two would just talk business and ignore everyone else. "Me and the kids were on the fringe," Linda Fuller said. "That wasn't my idea of family." In 1965 she told her husband that she was considering divorcing him, and she took an airplane to New York City to gain some space, talk to a pastor, and think about the future.

"It was a very quick success track. We made a lot of money and got everything that money gets for you: a Lincoln Continental, a cabin on the lake, two speedboats, 2,000 acres of land, 25 horses, hundreds of head of cattle, maids. We were living a fast and very successful life in terms of worldly standards. But the price you pay for that is that something has to give."

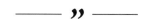

At the same time that his wife left, Fuller was suffering from breathing and other health problems that his doctor told him were stress related. When his wife left him, it was a wake-up call that his workaholic lifestyle was ruining everything he really cared about. "I lost my mother when I was three," he commented, "and now through my own stupidity I was about to lose my wife. It was a very sobering and shocking revelation for me." Determined not to let his family fall apart, he flew to New York to put his marriage back together. Meeting his wife, the two of them decided that they could remain married, but things would have to change—drastically. Then, while riding in a taxicab, Fuller suddenly had a revelation. "I think

Linda felt it too," he said of that moment. "It was nothing spooky or mysterious. I didn't hear any bells or choirs singing or anything like that. I just had a sensation of light. And I turned to Linda and I said, 'I think what we should do is leave business and give all our money away and make ourselves poor again and throw ourselves on God's mercy to find out what He wants to do with our lives. We've messed them up.'"

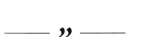

> *While riding in a taxicab, Fuller suddenly had a revelation. "I think Linda felt it too," he said of that moment. "It was nothing spooky or mysterious. I didn't hear any bells or choirs singing or anything like that. I just had a sensation of light. And I turned to Linda and I said, 'I think what we should do is leave business and give all our money away and make ourselves poor again and throw ourselves on God's mercy to find out what He wants to do with our lives. We've messed them up.'"*

Fuller had been a religious man all his life, but until that moment his Christian faith had always taken a back seat to his quest for money. But at that moment, his life was filled with religious purpose. His wife agreed wholeheartedly with his plan. Although their friends and family all thought he was crazy, Fuller sold his share of his business to Dees and proceeded to give all his money and possessions to charity. Immediately, he and Linda felt relieved. But the question then became: what to do next?

MAJOR INFLUENCES

The answer to their search for a new goal in life came unexpectedly from a man they had never heard of before: Clarence Jordan. Several weeks after deciding to abandon most of their worldly possessions, Fuller decided to visit a friend who lived at a Christian commune called Koinonia Farm near Americus, Georgia. Koinonia comes from the Greek word meaning "fellowship." The community was run by Clarence Jordan, a doctor of theology who founded Koinonia in order to create a community where Christians could live a simple country life in racial harmony. Fuller was immediately impressed with this man. Instead of just staying a few hours to meet his friend, he decided to stay at Koinonia for a month.

"Clarence Jordan thought more like Jesus than anybody I ever met," Fuller once said of the theologian. "I had never been exposed to the thinking that I was hearing from Clarence," he also said. "He said every character he read about in the Bible he met in Sumter County. I never thought like that. He related the Bible to now. So many Christians keep the Bible in some far distant past. He saw black people as totally equal and for a white boy that was totally revolutionary. He said everyone was made in God's image and his whole thinking was about unlimited love. Most people put limits on their love: 'I love MY wife, MY children, MY clan, MY race, MY nation.' Clarence said you have to take all the boundaries away."

But Jordan's ideas of racial tolerance outraged the local residents. Black residents were suspicious of the motives of this white man, and white residents despised Jordan's desire to have the two races living in the same community. There had been many incidents when the locals had burned down buildings and even fired guns at the commune. Koinonia was founded in 1942 with several dozen residents, but by the time the Fullers arrived there were only a few families left. Despite its lack of growth, Koinonia and its founder greatly impressed Fuller, who felt that Jordan's ideals, wisdom, and tolerance for others were the embodiment of Christianity. "I really believe that God brought me and Clarence together because Clarence was a big dreamer and I'm a practical man attracted to idealism," Fuller said. "Because of him, I've been able to weave those things together."

After having many conversations with Jordan, Fuller decided to find a worthwhile organization to work for, one whose goal wasn't just to make money. So in 1966 he took a position as development director at Tougaloo College in Mississippi, a nearly all-black college that was church supported. Working out of New York City, he helped raise funds for Tougaloo for two years, sometimes traveling around the world to do so. One trip in particular took him to Zaire (now the Democratic Republic of the Congo), where Fuller was appalled by the conditions of the shanty towns in which the people lived. He remembered that one of Jordan's dreams was to build decent housing for the poor, and this led his thoughts back to Koinonia.

CAREER HIGHLIGHTS

By the late 1960s, all of Fuller's skills and experiences — including his religious upbringing, his familiarity with construction, his business sense, and his desire to do something worthwhile with his life — finally came together in what would become his mission to help the less fortunate.

From Koinonia to Zaire

In 1968 Fuller and his family returned to Koinonia Farm. There, Jordan had an idea to create the Fund for Humanity, which would seek donations and use that money to help create self-sufficient farms where poor people

could live. Both Jordan and Fuller recognized that these people would need more than just farmland—they would need good homes. Together they established Koinonia Partners, which would build houses for low-income residents and give them no-interest loans. Fuller was named director of the new organization, and construction was started. Unfortunately, before the first building was completed, Jordan died of a heart attack on October 29, 1969. With the founder gone, Koinonia was managed by a board of directors. Fuller remained there for the next four years, helping to raise funds and working on public relations.

But Fuller was not content now that Jordan was gone, and so in 1973 he resigned his position at Koinonia and took his family to Mbandaka, Zaire, and the shantytowns he remembered there. "I was not at all happy with how things were being run [in Koinonia]," he recalled. "I discovered something about myself, and that was that I was not happy to be a part of something that I didn't have a very significant role in being the leader of. That inspired the move to Africa. I think it was a divine discontent." Beginning with a few thousand dollars donated by the Disciples of Christ Church, Fuller was challenged by the oppressive Zairian government, supply shortages, and difficult working conditions. Despite these problems, he managed to construct over 100 cement-block homes for the people there. He also set up funds to provide amputees with artificial legs and an eyeglass donation program where people in the United States would mail their used glasses to those who needed them in Zaire. He wrote about these experiences in his first book, *Bokotola*.

The Beginning of Habitat for Humanity International

After spending three years in Zaire, Fuller felt the urge to return to Georgia. Once back at Koinonia, he learned that the board of directors had decided to build homes only in the Americus area. This upset Fuller, who felt that their mission should not be limited to the local community, so he broke away from Koinonia to establish Habitat for Humanity International in 1976. Setting up an office in Americus in 1977, Fuller also started a law practice to earn some income for his family while working on Habitat.

The ambitious vision for Habitat is to provide descent housing for everyone who needs it — not just in the United States, but all over the world. But Fuller didn't want to establish a housing charity and just give people homes: he felt that most people, including the poor, don't really value

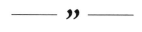

Fuller calls Habitat for Humanity the "economics of Jesus, or Bible economics. The Bible teaches if you lend money to the poor, not to charge interest. And so, we charge no interest. We add no profit, charge no interest, and that makes a house affordable to very low income families. Part of the economics of Jesus is also seen in the Bible where the laborers in the vineyard who work different amounts of time all got paid the same, not according to the amount they produced, but according to their need."

something that is provided for free. Instead, he wanted to give the poor affordable housing that was well built. So he created a non-profit organization where members would actually build homes. The construction work for Habitat is done almost entirely by volunteers, and much of the land and materials are donated. So Fuller was able to keep costs down. Low-income people who needed a home could then apply for a house, which could be purchased at a reduced rate and with a no-interest loan. Furthermore, the family that received the loan would have to assist with the construction of the house and promise to volunteer some of their time toward the building of homes for other people, something that Fuller calls "sweat equity." That helps the families feel like they've contributed to earning their homes.

Fuller working on a house for Habitat for Humanity.

Fuller calls his system the "economics of Jesus, or Bible economics. The Bible teaches if you lend money to the poor, not to charge interest. And so, we charge no interest. We add no profit, charge no interest, and that makes a house affordable to very low income families. Part of the economics of

Jesus is also seen in the Bible where the laborers in the vineyard who work different amounts of time all got paid the same, not according to the amount they produced, but according to their need." Fuller also added that "Habitat for Humanity is not charity. All we give away is an opportunity. The families have to help build their own houses." He also believes that providing better houses for the poor has other benefits, such as children doing better in school: "Their grades go up when you get them into a better living situation. Their health improves. Many poor families in this country are living in houses with lead-based paint, and that has the effect of dulling the brain, and children don't do well in school." Therefore, he has come to the conclusion that "building homes is not just good religion. . . . It's good politics, it's good sociology, it's good economics. It's just plain good common sense."

Controversy Turns to Support

Following the ideals of Clarence Jordan, Fuller set an ambitious goal for Habitat: to house every man, woman, and child on the planet who needed shelter. And he put no limits on race or religion, which offended many of the residents of Americus. In the early years of Habitat, Fuller had to overcome a great deal of prejudice and suspicion against his organization. Because Habitat built homes without the intention of making a profit, the Fullers were accused of being Communists, as well as being some sort of religious cult. His family was also harassed. When the Fullers first moved to Americus, broken glass was thrown on their driveway every day, and his children were shunned at school by the other kids. But Fuller fought back with kindness. Going through the local newspaper, he wrote congratulatory letters to residents about whom he had read positive stories in the paper, and he gradually won friends. Also, as Habitat grew, the organization began employing the townspeople. Slowly, people in Americus began to see Habitat as a good thing for their community.

> *"Habitat for Humanity is not charity. All we give away is an opportunity. The families have to help build their own houses."*

Jimmy Carter Lends a Hand

But Habitat got a real boost in public relations when, in 1984, former U.S. President Jimmy Carter announced that he and his wife, Rosalyn, would like to volunteer their support to Fuller's cause. Carter's home is in Plains, not far from Americus, and he had known about Koinonia and Habitat for years. In 1982 he publicly addressed Habitat's annual meeting, saying, "I am proud to be a neighbor of Koinonia. . . . To have seen, from perhaps too great a distance, the profound impact of Clarence Jordan. . . . I think I will be a better Christian because of Clarence Jordan, Koinonia, and Habitat. And I hope to grow the rest of my life with you." Lending his full support as a director, financial partner, and volunteer (Carter is a capable carpenter), Carter helped Fuller begin the Jimmy Carter Work Project, a once-a-year event in which Habitat holds a week-long building marathon on a particular project. The first of these was a renovation project in New York City, where the volunteers, including Jimmy and Rosalyn Carter, made an old 19-unit building suitable for new residents.

—— " ——

"[Children's] grades go up when you get them into a better living situation. Their health improves. Many poor families in this country are living in houses with lead-based paint, and that has the effect of dulling the brain, and children don't do well in school." Therefore, Fuller has come to the conclusion that "building homes is not just good religion. . . . It's good politics, it's good sociology, it's good economics. It's just plain good common sense."

—— " ——

Carter also helped Fuller in another, unexpected way. In 1990, Fuller found himself in a serious controversy when several women who had worked for Habitat accused him of sexual harassment. Fuller has always been an outwardly affectionate man, and he said that the contact he had made with these women had only been in the form of hugs. However, the women felt these gestures were inappropriate, and the board of directors wanted to strip Fuller of his powers as executive director of Habitat and place him in a more ceremonial role. Fuller, however, would have none of this, and he decided to resign.

After Fuller left, Habitat lost a $2 million line of credit. The organization began to suffer financial problems and ended up laying off 43 of its employees. Carter was angry over the board's decision, and he told them frankly that he would quit Habitat unless they reinstated Fuller. Under this kind of pressure, the members of the board relented and asked Fuller to return. However, he would no longer run the day-to-day operations of Habitat, a responsibility that now fell to executive vice president Jeff Snider, whom Fuller had hired for the role. Fuller is now president of Habitat and in charge of promoting the organization and being its spiritual

Former president Jimmy Carter and his wife, Rosalynn Carter, stand between Millard Fuller, left, and Leroy Troyer, right, leader of Habitat's Los Angeles Projects, as they review building plans for 20 houses in Los Angeles, June 1995.

center. From the harassment accusations he learned that, especially as a public figure, he had "to be more careful about who you touch and how you hug somebody, because the rules are different."

Amazing Growth

With the crisis of leadership behind it, Habitat for Humanity enjoyed a period of exponential growth during the 1990s. By 1995, the organization had constructed 12,000 homes, including 4,000 in the United States and 8,000 abroad. Fuller challenged Habitat and its many affiliates to push the limit and build more homes every year. The result was that by 2002, just seven years later, Habitat had multiplied its 1995 total ten times, completing 120,000 homes (including 20,000 in Africa) while expanding to 2,000 affiliate branches worldwide. Today, Habitat for Humanity continues to work toward its goal of housing the world's people. And Fuller's dream has already become a reality in Habitat's base in Sumter County, where every single shack has been replaced by a good quality home. In 1999, the organization launched its 21st Century Challenge, in which it asked all of its affiliates to do the same for their counties as the Americus headquarters did for Sumter County.

Although he gave up his fortune and material wealth, Fuller considers himself richer than ever before. He has won numerous awards, including several honorary doctoral degrees, but it is not for these honors that he works so hard. Rather, it is for the joy he and his wife have been able to bring to others. "I have had the experience," he said proudly, "of walking into the home of a family who had been living in a very bad situation and have the members of that family grab and hug me with tears pouring down their faces saying, 'You have made it possible to have a decent life.' What's that worth? It's priceless."

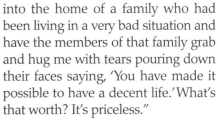

> "I have had the experience," Fuller said proudly, "of walking into the home of a family who had been living in a very bad situation and have the members of that family grab and hug me with tears pouring down their faces saying, 'You have made it possible to have a decent life.' What's that worth? It's priceless."

MARRIAGE AND FAMILY

Fuller married Linda Caldwell on August 30, 1959. The two originally met while he was a junior in law school and she was a junior in high school. She has a degree in elementary education and, as part of a special Habitat mission, she currently focuses on providing homes for those who are struggling with mental diseases. They have four children: Christopher, who is a pastor; Kimberly, who is a flight attendant; Faith, who is a television newscaster; and Georgia, who is a teacher. For years, the family lived in one of the Habitat-built homes in a low-income area of Americus, but recently they moved into a larger home in a better area.

WRITINGS

Bokotola, 1978
Love in the Mortar Joints: The Story of Habitat for Humanity, 1980 (With Diane Scott)
No More Shacks: The Daring Vision of Habitat for Humanity, 1986
The Excitement Is Building: How Habitat for Humanity Is Putting Roofs over Heads and Hope in Hearts, 1990
The Theology of the Hammer, 1994

A Simple, Decent Place to Live, 1995

More than Houses, 1999

Cotton Patch for the Kingdom: Clarence Jordan's Demonstration Plot at Koinonia Farm, 2002 (With Ann Louise Coble)

Building Materials for Life: Radical Common Sense, the Power of Right Thinking, Persistence, Plowing New Ground, Relevant Religion, and 35 Other Essays on How to Enhance Your Life, 2002

AWARDS AND HONORS

Clarence Jordan Exemplary Christian Service Award (Southern Baptist Theological Seminary): 1986

Dr. Martin Luther King Jr. Humanitarian Award (Martin Luther King Jr. Center): 1987

Distinguished Christian Service in Social Welfare Award (North American Association of Christians in Social Work): 1988

International Humanity Service Award (American Overseas Association): 1989

Public Service Achievement Award (Common Cause): 1989

M. Justin Herman Memorial Award (National Association of Housing and Development Officials): 1989

Temple Award for Creative Altruism: 1990

Professional Achievement Award (Partnership for Affordable Housing): 1993

Harry S. Truman Public Service Award (City of Independence, Missouri): 1994

Builder of the Year (*Professional Builders Magazine*): 1995

Faithful Servant Award (National Association of Evangelicals): 1996

Spirit of Georgia Award: 1996

National Housing Hall of Fame: 1996

Presidential Medal of Freedom (United States Government): 1996

Jefferson Award: 1999, for outstanding contributions to his community

Mark O. Hatfield Leadership Award (Council for Christian Colleges and Universities): 2001, for demonstrating uncommon leadership that reflects values of Christian higher education

FURTHER READING

Books

Contemporary Heroes and Heroines, Vol. 3, 1998

Encyclopedia of World Biography Supplement, Vol. 18, 1998

Who's Who in America, 2002

Periodicals

Boston Globe, Dec. 28, 1997, National/Foreign section, p.A1
Chicago Tribune, May 14, 1995, WomanNews section, p.3
Christian Science Monitor, Apr. 9, 1986, p.7; Aug. 7, 1987, p.21; Dec. 28, 1990, p.13
Christianity Today, June 14, 1999, p.44; June 10, 2002, p.28
Current Biography Yearbook, 1995
Los Angeles Times, Aug. 6, 1988, part 2, p.7; Nov. 4, 2001, p.E2
National Review, Dec. 30, 1988, p.40
New York Times, May 25, 1982, p.A16; Sep. 3, 1984, section 1, p.1
Time, Jan. 16, 1989, p.12

Online Database

Biography Resource Center Online, 2003, articles *Contemporary Heroes and Heroines,* 1998, and *Encyclopedia of World Biography Supplement,* 1998

ADDRESS

Millard Fuller
Habitat for Humanity International
121 Habitat Street
Americus, GA 31709-3498

WORLD WIDE WEB SITE

http://www.habitat.org

Jeanette Lee 1971-

American Professional Pool Player Known as
"The Black Widow"
The Most Visible and Popular Women's Pool Player
in the World

BIRTH

Jeanette Lee was born on July 9, 1971, in Brooklyn, New York.
She was the younger of two girls born to Bo Chun Lee, who
owned a tobacco shop, and Sonya Lee, who worked as a nurse.
Her parents had been born in Korea and immigrated to the
United States. When Jeanette was five years old, her father left

———— " ————

"People don't know what scoliosis does to those who have it. It just destroys your self-esteem, going to school in a cast or a brace looking like a monster and having no one to talk to who can understand and support you. A huge part of my [own] healing process was learning to feel good about myself and turn that part of my life into a positive...."

———— " ————

the family and returned to Korea. She had no further contact with him until she visited Korea as an adult. Her mother eventually remarried, and from that time on Jeanette and her older sister were raised by their step-father.

YOUTH

The Lee family had very little money and lived in one of Brooklyn's tough neighborhoods. In fact, Jeanette often got beaten up for being one of the few Koreans in the neighborhood.

Lee's family tried to combine the cultural traditions of Korea with those of their new homeland. For example, they emphasized the Korean value of hard work as well as the American vision of opportunity. The Lees dreamed of a future in which Jeanette completed school and then married a Korean doctor.

Her parents were bilingual, meaning that they spoke two languages, English and Korean, but Jeanette spoke only English. Growing up she felt closest to her grandmother, even though her grandmother spoke only Korean. Her stepfather worked long days and Jeanette did not get to spend much time with him. But she respected him because he made her mother happy.

Lee was a shy child, but she had a strong competitive streak. She rebelled against her parents' strict rules as she got older. For example, she began wearing her trademark all-black outfits in her youth because it upset her mother. When she was 11, Jeanette moved out of her family's house and lived with a variety of friends and one of her teachers before eventually returning home.

At the age of 13, Jeanette was diagnosed with scoliosis, a medical condition that causes the spine to curve. It's a spinal deformity that most often appears during adolescence. Her mother first noticed the S-shaped curve in her back when the family was at the beach. That started a very tough time for Jeanette. She went through eight surgeries and had metal rods inserted into her spine to keep it straight. Afterward, she had to wear a back brace and was unable to play sports with her friends and schoolmates. She also had to wear thick glasses to correct her terrible eyesight, which was so poor that she was classified as legally blind.

Lee later said that these things made her feel like a "monster" during her teen years. Her competitive nature made it even more difficult for her to handle these physical limitations. She ended up spending a lot of time playing cards when she was young because it provided an outlet for her competitiveness.

EDUCATION

Lee was an excellent student and was accepted to the prestigious Bronx Science School in New York. For many years, she dreamed of becoming an elementary school teacher. The details of her education are unclear, but it appears that she dropped out of the Bronx Science School before graduating and earned her high school diploma elsewhere. She later attended Queens College, but she dropped out before earning a degree in order to focus on pool.

CHOOSING A CAREER

Lee first played pool at camp at the age of ten. She also accompanied a few boyfriends to pool halls over the years. But it was only after she saw "The Color of Money"—a 1989 movie about a pair of professional pool players (portrayed by Paul Newman and Tom Cruise)—that she became truly intrigued by the game. Lee went to a local pool hall called Chelsea Billiards to check it out first hand. While there she was mesmerized by the play of Johnny Ervolino, an older regular at the club who was poetry in motion on the pool table.

Lee's deep fascination with the game of pool began when she was 18 years old. At this point in her life, she had dropped out of college and was

— " —

"When you're young, you don't know why things happen to you. But if anything good comes out of this, it's when you learn that you can overcome it and perhaps be an inspiration to someone out there who is going through something similar. They're going to know that there is at least one person they can talk to and realize that you're not offering them pity, you're offering them inspiration."

— " —

working at a series of odd jobs. For example, she worked as an editorial assistant in a Korean computer company and as a hostess at a rhythm and blues club in Manhattan. "I was an aimless party girl who woke up every morning wishing I could be anybody but who I was," she recalled. "Then I discovered pool. And once I did, I was not to be stopped. Before pool, I had no reason to wake up in the morning, and after pool there is not enough time in the world." Pool was a sport Lee could play despite her bad back, and as she improved her pool-playing skills she developed the self-confidence she had lacked as a child.

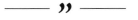

"I honestly don't think it matters if your passion is pool or business or building a family or all three. What matters is that you find the strength and the courage and the means to achieve your goal."

Within two months Lee was playing pool for money. She started out hustling tables at pool halls, meaning that she accepted challenges to play against other people with bets riding on the outcome. According to one tale from these early days, Lee once won $90,000 in a 23-hour period by taking wagers from challengers.

For many years, she played pool nearly every night of the week. For the record, Lee claims that she never "sand-bagged," or pretended to be a poor player in order to set up men to be beaten. However, she admits that most men's egos were so big that they did not believe any woman—no matter how good—could beat them. And she gladly took advantage of this foolish notion since she needed the money to survive.

Learning to play pool was hard work for Lee. She practiced every day, sometimes more than 15 hours a day. She once played non-stop for 37 hours, although she was in such pain afterward that her friends had to carry her home. She even slept with her hand taped in the cue bridge position (the way the hand sits on the pool table to prop the cue stick steadily). While Lee gained both the skills and the mental toughness necessary to be a champion, she also began to learn some important lessons about life. "I honestly don't think it matters if your passion is pool or business or building a family or all three," she explained. "What matters is that you find the strength and the courage and the means to achieve your goal."

Within five years, Lee was the top-ranked female pool player in the world. As she wrote in her book *The Black Widow's Guide to Killer Pool*, "I could have quit a thousand times, after bitter losses, close calls, and hospital vis-

Lee in action during a tournament in Minneapolis, February 1996.

its, but I never did, because in my heart I knew I could make it, even though everyone else thought it was unrealistic." At first, Lee's parents did not support her decision to become a professional pool player. They worried about her staying out late into the night and hanging out at pool halls where most of the patrons were men. But when she started winning tournaments, her mother conceded, "You know, as much as we think you're fooling around the pool room, you can't win all these tournaments unless you've really been working."

CAREER HIGHLIGHTS

"The Black Widow" Emerges

Lee turned professional in 1993. Women's pool (or billiards) tournaments are organized by the Women's Professional Billiard Association (WPBA). This organization sponsors a number of tournaments around the world each year. Participants earn points based on their finish at each professional tournament, and they are ranked each month based on their total points over the preceding 12-month period. Many professional pool players also take part in other tournaments sponsored by pool halls, casinos, and resorts. Although these tournaments do not count toward the WPBA rankings, they do offer prize money.

Shortly after turning pro, Lee earned the nickname "The Black Widow." The nickname was partly based on her jet black hair, all-black attire at tournaments, and sleek look. But the name was also appropriate from a competitive standpoint, because she often devoured her opponents the way a black widow spider eats its mate. The nickname originally came from Gabe Vigorito, the owner of the Howard Beach Billiard Club. He once said that "Jeanette walked in as a beautiful, young thing but when she started shooting, she killed her opponent. She went from a butterfly to a black widow." The nickname remained a private joke until Lee let it slip to a reporter who then used it in the *New York Times*. Lee's mother tried to change her nickname to "The Lily of the Valley," but "The Black Widow" fit Lee's mystique, and the name stuck.

> "You have to figure out what happened," she reflected about a tough tournament loss. "Don't ignore the wound and hope it closes by itself. If you do, you'll be left with a terrible scar. Use pain as your motivation — not just to get angry, but to do something about it. I won the next tournament, and the one after that, and by the end of the next year I was the number-one-ranked professional in the world. And it wouldn't have happened without that loss in Germany."

Unfortunately for Lee, her nickname only added to the negative perceptions of her held by other players. They initially viewed Lee as aggressive and cocky, and they did not particularly like her. She earned some of the criticism by stomping around after missing shots, and glaring at both the table and her opponents. She also once stated early in her career that she wanted to be the best and intended to crush anyone who got in her way. But some fellow players resented her simply because she was young, attractive, fashionable, ambitious, and highly competitive.

Rising to the Top

Lee made a splash almost immediately upon joining the WPBA tour, when she took second place at the 1993 World Championships in Konigswinter, Germany. She also learned a great deal in this important tournament. Lee was on fire early in the competition, sinking difficult shot after difficult shot. Her confidence irritated players who were more experienced than her. Although Lee had worked hard and practiced thousands of hours, she was still considered a rookie who had not yet paid her dues.

As Lee advanced through the tournament, other players started booing her. In the first set of the finals—in which the winner had to take two out of three sets—Lee got flustered and was blown out by her opponent, Loree Jon Jones. Lee then realized that she was playing right into the hands of her tormentors, and she regrouped to dominate the second set. As the crowd geared up to watch the deciding third set, however, she panicked. As she thought about how significant it was that she was playing for the world championship as a 23-year-old rookie, a flood of nervousness washed over her. Lee was unable to shake these feelings, and Jones easily won the decisive third set to claim the championship.

But Lee was wise enough to learn from that event and apply what she learned to her future play. "You have to figure out what happened," she explained. "Don't ignore the wound and hope it closes by itself. If you do, you'll be left with a terrible scar. Use pain as your motivation—not just to get angry, but to do something about it. I won the next tournament, and the one after that, and by the end of the next year I was the number-one-ranked professional in the world. And it wouldn't have happened without that loss in Germany."

In 1993 Lee moved to Reno, Nevada, where there were more competitive pool opportunities. In 1994 she won five of the 12 WPBA tournaments and rose into the top 10 in the WPBA rankings. She also won the U.S. Open Championships and took second place for the second consecutive year in the WPBA World Championships. These accomplishments earned her the WPBA's Player of the Year award.

In 1995, less than two years after turning pro, Lee became the top-ranked female pool player in the world. In 1998, following multiple tournament wins, she was named the WPBA Sportsperson of the Year. In 1999 Lee played as the in-house professional at the Amsterdam Billiard Club for the National Straight Pool Championship. (In straight pool, players shoot for all 15 balls, each of which is worth a point.) She was one of only two women competing in the tournament against 80 men. In one round of the tournament she played Johnny Ervolino—the old man who inspired her ten years earlier with his fluid play—and she beat him.

Taking a Break

Although Lee had a successful year in 1999, she struggled against severe back pain throughout the season. She decided to take the first half of 2000 off in order to undergo more back surgery. Over the course of her career, Lee has had surgery on her neck, shoulder, and back, for herniated discs, tendinitis, and a tumor. She also had the metal rod that had been inserted in her back when she was a teenager replaced. Because of these rods she cannot lean forward at more than an 80 degree angle, which is barely far enough to break on a billiard table. This limitation makes her status as one of the world's top pool players even more remarkable.

During her time off from pool, Lee co-authored a book called *The Black Widow's Guide to Killer Pool.* She had the following advice for women who want to become professional pool players: "You have to understand the level of commitment that goes towards being a top pro. You have to know that it's going to be tough out there, and unless you love it more than anything, you're not going to make it. You have to have a tough mind, and you have to be willing to take hard losses, so when you overcome them, the win is so great. Stay focused and no matter what gets you down, just believe in your heart whatever your dreams are. Set real goals and be willing to back it up with hard work."

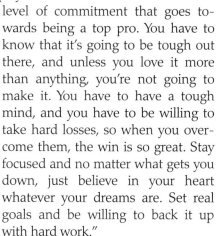

"I have learned how to compete, how to lose gracefully and win frequently. I have come to understand the psychology of success, the importance of mental toughness. I have learned the difference between competing against men and against women. I know how to stay focused under pressure, and how to achieve goals in the face of seemingly impossible odds."

Back to the Game

The layoff from the tournament circuit caused Lee to drop to number five in the world rankings. She returned in the second half of 2000 determined to reclaim her number one spot, but she failed to win any tournaments that year. In 2001, however, Lee came back to win a gold medal at the World Games in Akita, Japan. This marked the first time that pool was included in the World Games, which is the first step for the sport to gain official recognition for the Olympic Games. Lee also placed in the top 10 in five of the six tournaments she entered that year.

Lee was honored when ESPN voted her the third-sexiest female athlete in the world behind track star Marion Jones and tennis player Anna Kournikova. "I think women should be very proud to be women and celebrate their femininity, and that's something that I do," she stated. "I'm very

Lee lines up a shot during a guest appearance at an exhibition in Boston, February 2001.

proud to be a woman. I want to be feminine and still be able to be great and hold myself with class and dignity, and that's what I try to do."

Because of her good looks and aggressive style of play, Lee has become a prominent personality in the pool world and beyond. She has appeared on a number of television programs, including "Good Morning America," "Extra," "Hard Copy," and "MTV Sports," as well as in such publications as *People, Glamour,* and *Sports Illustrated.* "I think I've opened up a lot of eyes," she noted. "I've brought a lot of media attention to the sport [of pool], in a very positive way. It was thought of as Men's Pool. I represent Women's Billiards and it is awesome and cool and fun. I do take some credit for that."

Lee is the highest-earning pool player in the world today. Thanks to her exotic beauty, fierce attitude in competition, and diligent effort, she has earned several endorsement deals that bring in 90 percent of her income. Lee has appeared in advertisements for whiskey and for pool gloves and equipment (through a major long-term deal with Imperial International). She also developed her own line of pool cues and an Interplay video game. In addition,

Lee is a model, actress, and motivational speaker. She has appeared in the HBO TV series "Arliss," the movie *The Other Sister*, and a commercial for ESPN's "SportsCenter."

Lee has worked hard to change the arrogant reputation she acquired early in her professional career. She has grown and learned from her experiences over the years. "I have learned how to compete, how to lose gracefully and win frequently," she said. "I have come to understand the psychology of success, the importance of mental toughness. I have learned the difference between competing against men and against women. I know how to stay focused under pressure, and how to achieve goals in the face of seemingly impossible odds."

> "I've grown up a lot. I know more about how to deal with the other players and the press, and how to handle myself at tournaments. But some things haven't changed — the World Nine-Ball Championship isn't a Miss Congeniality contest sponsored by Martha Stewart. And I'm not out there looking to make friends. I'm still looking to kick butt and take names."

At the same time, Lee remains a fierce competitor with supreme confidence in her abilities. "I've grown up a lot," she noted. "I know more about how to deal with the other players and the press, and how to handle myself at tournaments. But some things haven't changed — the World Nine-Ball Championship isn't a Miss Congeniality contest sponsored by Martha Stewart. And I'm not out there looking to make friends. I'm still looking to kick butt and take names." Lee's outgoing and flamboyant personality make her a crowd favorite. She lets her emotions show whether she is playing well or not, sharing her passion and her pain with fans.

Lee credits attitude as the determining factor that separates a true champion from a good pool shooter. "It's all about meeting the challenge," she stated. "Because life does not just line up for you to conquer it. If it were that easy, we wouldn't need 80 years to get it right. The essence of competition is pushing your limits, testing yourself against the best. That is the best way to improve, and the only way to become a champion. If you don't have that attitude, you might as well pack your bags. Even if you win the tournament against watered-down competition, you are never going to get anywhere in life ducking challenge after challenge."

As of January 2003, Lee ranked fourth in the WPBA based on the number of points earned in major tournaments over the previous year. And she shows no signs of slowing down. "I love playing pool and I don't see myself stopping anytime soon — at least not until I get back to being number one in the world again," she said. "If I have to, I'll use my cue as a cane to get around the table. Just as long as I can keep playing." Lee wants to leave her mark on history as the best pool player who ever lived. She also hopes to earn enough money to help her parents retire and put her cousins through college.

Billards player Jeanette Lee attends the Women's Sport Foundation Annual Gala in New York City, October 15, 2001.

MARRIAGE AND FAMILY

In 1996 Lee married fellow professional pool player George Breedlove (nicknamed "The Flamethrower" because of his strong breaks), whom she met at a tournament in Los Angeles. Breedlove proposed marriage after just three dates with Lee. They currently live in a large ranch house in Indianapolis, Indiana, with George's two teenage daughters, Morgan and Olivia. They are hoping to have more children in the future, although doctors are concerned that Lee's back is not strong enough for her to carry a child to term. She can have corrective surgery in the future to improve her chances of a successful pregnancy, but she would have to give up her professional career to do so.

Breedlove no longer plays pool professionally and has started a business making custom furniture. The couple has promised each other never to be apart for more than seven days, and Lee calls her husband every day that she's away. She admits that Breedlove's best game is better than hers, but says that she can beat him when he is not focused on playing up to his full potential.

HOBBIES AND OTHER INTERESTS

Lee works out every day with a personal trainer. In addition to trying to maintain flexibility in her back, she also works on breathing and upper arm strength. She also practices pool six to eight hours a day and travels up to 300 days a year.

When she's not practicing pool, Lee likes to play with the kids in her neighborhood or with her dog, Sandy, and cat, Lucky. Her favorite non-pool sports to play are golf and bowling. She also enjoys going to the spa and shopping for make-up and clothes (she especially likes shoes and purses). She has also taken up painting, another activity she can pursue despite her bad back.

Lee is involved in charitable activities that mirror her own personal experiences. She is a national spokesperson and vice president of the board of directors for the Scoliosis Association. She also established the Jeanette Lee Foundation in 1998 to raise money for scoliosis research.

"People don't know what scoliosis does to those who have it," said Lee. "It just destroys your self-esteem, going to school in a cast or a brace looking like a monster and having no one to talk to who can understand and support you. A huge part of my [own] healing process was learning to feel good about myself and turn that part of my life into a positive. When you're young, you don't know why things happen to you. But if anything good comes out of this, it's when you learn that you can overcome it and perhaps be an inspiration to someone out there who is going through something similar. They're going to know that there is at least one person they can talk to and realize that you're not offering them pity, you're offering them inspiration."

Lee is also on the board of the Billiard Education Foundation, which encourages young people to get a good education and allows them to earn money for college through playing pool. She also promotes causes on behalf of women athletes on the Diverse Races Committee of the Women's Sports Foundation. She recently met with President George W. Bush at the White House to fight for equal funding for men's and women's college sports. Finally, Lee is an active member of the WPBA board, which is responsible for the rules and regulations of professional billiards.

WRITINGS

The Black Widow's Guide to Killer Pool, 2000 (with Adam Scott Gershenson)

HONORS AND AWARDS

WPBA Player of the Year (*Billiards Digest*): 1994
WPBA Player of the Year (*Billiards Magazine*): 1994
World Billiards Championships: 1994, silver medal; 1995, silver medal

WPBA Sportsperson of the Year Award: 1998
Akita World Games: 1999, gold medal
Billiard Congress of America Open Nine-Ball Champion: 2001

FURTHER READING

Books

Lee, Jeanette. *The Black Widow's Guide to Killer Pool*, 2000 (with Adam Scott Gershenson)

Periodicals

Chicago Daily Herald, Jan. 12, 2002, Sports sec., p.1
Current Biography Yearbook, 2002
Daily Telegraph (London), Mar. 19, 1997, p.69
Indianapolis Star, Feb. 21, 1999, p.J1; June 3, 2000, p.E2
Oregonian, Jan. 17, 2002, p.D1
People, Mar. 13, 1995, p.86
Sports Illustrated, July 8, 1996, p.7
St. Petersburg Times, Feb. 18, 2002, p.D1
USA Today, Mar. 12, 1997, p.C2

ADDRESSES

Jeanette Lee Foundation
1427 West 86th Street
Suite 183
Indianapolis, IN 46260

Scoliosis Association
P.O. Box 811705
Boca Raton, FL 33481
Phone: 800-800-0669

WORLD WIDE WEB SITES

http://www.jeanettelee.tv
http://www.scoliosis-assoc.org
http://www.womenssportsfoundation.org
http://womensportsonline.com

Clint Mathis 1976-

American Professional Soccer Player
Forward for the New York/New Jersey MetroStars and
for the U.S. National Team

BIRTH

Clint Mathis was born on November 25, 1976, in Conyers,
Georgia. He is the son of Pat Mathis, who works as a bank
manager, and Phil Mathis, a former preacher who is currently
an insurance salesman. Pat and Phil Mathis divorced in 1988,
when Clint was about 12. The youngest of four children, Clint
has two older brothers and an older sister.

YOUTH

According to his parents, Mathis was born to be an athlete. "As soon as he was born I said, 'Oh, my gosh, he looks like a ballplayer,'" said his mother. He was walking from the time he was just nine months old, and he was already playing with a soccer ball when he was three. His mother quickly realized that her son had great potential in the sport. "I used to take him to the field in his stroller to watch his brothers," she remembered. "He just started walking. Then he was kicking paper cups, balls of paper, whatever. It's like he always played." She added, "When Clint was a little bitty thing, I told him, 'I feel like God has given you a gift.' He had such knowledge so young. He was four and yelling at other kids about being offsides."

Mathis played with his soccer ball indoors and out. A favorite family story relates how he used to kick the ball against a curio cabinet. He would break the glass so often that, after a while, the repairman stopped charging the family for the glass. His brothers also played soccer, so when Clint got a little older, they were his first coaches. In the backyard, they made their younger brother maneuver the soccer ball using only his left foot. Like most people, Mathis is right-handed and right-footed, so the purpose of the exercise was to make him equally adept using either foot. Because the rules of soccer prohibit using your hands to touch the ball, the ability to use both feet is crucial. The young boy also imaginatively invented a game he called "soccer croquet" in which he had to kick the ball between multiple obstacles. This helped him develop dexterity.

> "
>
> *"I used to take him to the field in his stroller to watch his brothers," his mother remembered. "He just started walking. Then he was kicking paper cups, balls of paper, whatever. It's like he always played. . . . When Clint was a little bitty thing, I told him, 'I feel like God has given you a gift.' He had such knowledge so young. He was four and yelling at other kids about being offsides."*
>
> "

Mathis's current coach for the MetroStars, Octavio Zambrano, believes that this type of unstructured practice helped him become the player he is today: "[In the U.S.] we have a system where we have youth soccer leagues, where young players are constantly being coached and supervised by adults who often have very little experience in soccer. Clint grew up playing the game in a different environment than most Americans, in one that resembled much more my own youth in Ecuador. That form of play allows for the growth of creativity, for imagination to flourish, and you see that in what Clint does. In a sense, he grew up in a pure soccer culture that does not yet exist in this country."

By the time he was five, Mathis was playing magnet ball, a kind of simplified soccer for little kids. When he was nine, his mother received an invitation in the mail for her son to become part of an Olympic development team. Pat Mathis was a single mother raising four children by working multiple jobs — at the time, she worked in a dentist's office, cleaned houses, and sold jewelry and antiques. So she didn't have very much money to spend on traveling around the country so her son could play soccer. However, she was determined not to let money stop her, and cut back on every expense she could. Other parents, she said, "didn't know I was eating crackers and Coke in the room for dinner." But the sacrifices she made would prove to be well worth it.

> *"Clint loved every sport, but after that . . . he'd say he was going to play basketball, then [he'd say], 'Well, that might mess up my soccer, I'd better not.' He played basketball for fun. Soccer was way too serious."*

CHOOSING A CAREER

Besides soccer, Mathis played other sports, including football, when he was a little kid. But when he was just nine years old he saw something that inspired him to focus on soccer. When he was watching television one day, he saw the World Cup quarterfinal game between the national teams for England and Argentina. One of the stars of the Argentine team, Diego Maradona, made two brilliant goals that led to a victory for his country. One goal has since become known to soccer fans as the legendary "Hand of God" goal. Mathis later recalled, "I saw Diego Maradona dribbling through seven or eight guys [when he scored]. Not the 'Hand of God' goal, but the other goal. It was amazing. I said, 'Man, I want to do that.'" Although soccer still wasn't a big sport in America, he said "that is when I first realized how big the World Cup was around the world."

Mathis became a devoted Maradona fan, and he loved the Maradona jersey that his mother bought for him. "He wore it night and day," she said, adding that "Clint loved every sport, but after that . . . he'd say he was going to play basketball, then [he'd say], 'Well, that might mess up my soccer, I'd better not.' He played basketball for fun. Soccer was way too serious."

EDUCATION

Mathis was a bright student who started high school one year earlier than most teens, but what he enjoyed most about school was, of course, playing soccer. As a teenager, he attended Heritage High School in Conyers, Georgia, where he was on the varsity team and impressed his coach, Karl Bostick. "I've seen him play twice and he took four shots. He scored four goals," Bostick said in 1994. "I have no doubt he's the best scorer in the state. He rockets everything." Mathis was the lead scorer on his team, leading it to two state champion-

ships in 1992 and 1993, and he was named "Georgia Player of the Year." But he didn't stop there. In addition to his high school team, he also played for the South Metro Lightning, which won a state championship, the State Select Team, and the U.S. National Junior Team, all while still getting good grades and graduating in 1994.

Not surprisingly, Mathis was recruited by many colleges and universities. He accepted a scholarship from the University of South Carolina to begin the next chapter of his up-and-coming career. At USC he studied exercise science and, of course, played soccer for the USC Gamecocks. He also played soccer for a U.S. Youth Soccer Association team called the Lightning Soccer Club, which went to its first national championship with Mathis as a star player, and he was on the U.S. Under-20 National Team in 1995. In the meantime, at USC he scored 53 goals from 1994 to 1997, had 15 assists, was named All-American twice, and was nominated three times for the Hermann Trophy for best college player — like a soccer version of the Heisman Trophy in football. He helped the Gamecocks go to the NCAA Tournament in 1995, and the USC team was ranked among the top five university soccer teams while he was there. In 1997, he also played for Team USA, which won a bronze medal at the World University Games in Italy. Mathis might have accomplished even more during his college years, had he not injured his knee in 1996. Despite missing some games, his record at USC demonstrated that he was professional material.

CAREER HIGHLIGHTS

When Mathis entered the world of professional soccer in 1998, the sport was just barely beginning to attract the attention of Americans, who have never been as enthusiastic about soccer as the rest of the world. Mathis would soon help to change all that.

A Brief History of Soccer

The game of soccer, which is more commonly called "football" outside the United States, was invented in England in the third century A.D. The game was first organized under the London Football Association in 1863 and became popular in continental Europe. In 1904, with soccer spreading throughout Europe, the Federation Internationale de Football Association (FIFA) was created to standardize rules and regulate international competition. Today, soccer is the most popular sport around the world. There are hotly competitive leagues in Europe and in South America, in particular. Children there grow up cheering their favorite soccer teams, rather than football, baseball, or basketball teams.

Meanwhile, in the United States, American "football," which actually more closely resembles the English game of rugby, was becoming a popular sport. In the U.S., American football quickly gained many more fans than soccer, which was regarded as a less exciting, foreign sport. Nevertheless soccer grew in popularity among children and teens in the 1980s and 1990s, and a movement began to grow to create professional leagues. The North American Soccer League was formed, and in 1996, Major League Soccer was established with 12 professional teams. Americans were beginning to get interested in the World Cup, which is the international soccer competition played once every four years. Countries around the world form national teams from their best players. Teams play in a series of qualifying games to get into the World Cup, and only 32 teams qualify. Those teams compete in a month-long competition of elimination. The World Cup is the most popular sporting event in the world. The American men's team has been very weak, and it rarely even qualified to play for the Cup. In 1998 the men's national team finished dead last in the competition. Happier news came from the U.S. women's team, however, which won world championships in 1991 in China and in 1999 in Brazil. But America was yearning to show that it could have a world-class men's team, too.

Playing for the Los Angeles Galaxy, Mathis takes the ball down field in this game against the Dallas Burn, March 1999.

The Los Angeles Galaxy

After finishing college, Mathis was immediately drafted in 1998 by the Los Angeles Galaxy, a Major League Soccer team. Excelling at passing the ball, free kicks, and wild, risk-taking goals, the young player was a top-scoring rookie who helped his team go to the MLS Cup final in 1999. Although easygoing off the field, he gained a reputation for being a loose cannon on the field who had a highly unconventional playing style. "When I play," Mathis once said, "I like to try to catch people off guard. People don't expect the unexpected, and that's what I try to do. You can call it arrogance or confidence. I call it competitiveness. I wouldn't want to be on the field if I could accept losing." He also continued to develop a reputation—begun in college—for being a bit of a showboat. Sometimes he will take his shirt off after scoring a goal (something for which he has been penalized) or do a victory "worm dance" where he flops on the ground on his stomach and bounces up and down. Mathis at times also lets his temper get the best of him, and he has been ejected from games for yelling at officials. "I'm a nice guy off the field," he said, "but on it, I guess you could say I'm [a jerk] out there."

———— " ————

"When I play, I like to try to catch people off guard. People don't expect the unexpected, and that's what I try to do. You can call it arrogance or confidence. I call it competitiveness. I wouldn't want to be on the field if I could accept losing."

———— " ————

Mathis was unique among professional soccer players in America at the start of his career because, at the time, many teams were still recruiting players from other countries who were more skilled at the game. Because of his Southern background, accent, and goofy sense of humor his teammates jokingly nicknamed him "Cletus," implying that he was a backwoods bumpkin. Yet "Cletus" chalked up an outstanding record with the Galaxy, scoring 43 goals in the regular season from 1998 to 2000.

In 1998, the same year Mathis joined the Galaxy, the U.S. national team's star player Claudio Reyna was injured. That created an open spot on the National team roster, and Mathis was selected to fill it. Although he didn't get much playing time during his first two years with the national team, Mathis was voted MVP in a game against Australia in 1998 and scored his first goal in 2000 in a World Cup qualifying game against Barbados. But despite his record, the Galaxy team left him unprotected in 2000 so that they could obtain Mexican player Luis Hernandez. This meant that any team in the MLS could snatch up Mathis, which is just what the New York/New Jersey MetroStars did.

Playing for the New York/New Jersey MetroStars, Mathis dribbles the ball during a game against the Los Angeles Galaxy, August 2002.

The New York/New Jersey MetroStars

MetroStars coach Octavio Zambrano was happy to acquire Mathis for his roster in 2000. "It was clear to me that he was one of the best on the field, if not the best," said Zambrano. "I thought he would go earlier [in the draft]. I was extremely surprised—and ecstatic." Mathis was happy as well, because he didn't get as much playing time as he wanted with the Galaxy and was moved around a lot to different positions. "I have a lot more freedom [with the MetroStars]," he said. "This is the first time I've had a solid position [as a forward]. That gives me confidence, and more freedom to produce chances for the team." And even though he came from a small-town background, Mathis enjoyed New York City and soon purchased a newly built townhouse in nearby New Jersey. To show his appreciation for his fans with his new team, when he scored his first goal against his former Galaxy teammates as a MetroStar he took off his jersey to reveal a T-shirt that said "I Love New York." It was a gesture that his new fans really appreciated.

In 2000, Mathis scored 16 goals and had 14 assists, won the Honda MVP/Budweiser Scoring Championship, and set an MLS single-game record by scoring five goals in one match. The 2001 season, therefore, seemed to hold a lot of promise for the young star. He was excited to keep playing for the MetroStars, but at the same time something even bigger was looming over the horizon: the 2002 World Cup.

World Cup Hopes

During the first half of 2001, everything was going great for Mathis. Every game he played for the MetroStars ended in either a victory or a tie. In one game, he scored a hat trick in a 4-1 victory over the Kansas City Wizards, using his head, his right foot, and his left foot to score goals. In another game, he rocketed 60 yards, weaving past Dallas Burn defenders to score what *Sports Illustrated* called "one of the most electrifying strikes in United States soccer. The goal, the replays of which were aired worldwide, . . . evoked heady comparisons to Maradona." Mathis said that "I try to play on instinct. I just go. The moment I start thinking on the field is the moment I start messing up."

Mathis was also a valued player on the National Team, assisting his team to a victory over Mexico in February and beating the Honduras team in March. With his success in the United States, he began to eye prospects in Europe, where the competition was more intense and the pay much better. He had aspirations to join one of the Premier League teams in England because he liked the way the English played soccer—fast, just like him. If he could get a playing spot there, he could triple his American salary of about $200,000 a year, even if he spent all his time on the bench. However, Mathis had a contract with MLS and the MetroStars that didn't expire until 2003, and the star player was unlikely to be released from his obligation.

Bad news came in June 2001 when Mathis tore his right anterior cruciate ligament (ACL), a critical tendon behind the knee. The injury put him out of action for the rest of the year. Despite being sidelined with this injury, though, he was still making news in the media. In May 2002 Mathis was featured on the covers of *Sports Illustrated* and *ESPN: The Magazine,* the first American men's soccer player to have done so.

On the eve of the 2002 World Cup, many viewed Mathis as a potential savior for American soccer. According to Jeff Z. Klein in the *New York Times,* "What makes Mathis such a prized commodity is his ability to create goals at any time and from any place on the field, the rarest and most precious skill in a sport where a final score of 2-1 reflects a fiesta of rollicking, high-octane offense. No American has ever scored at such a prolific rate as Mathis over the past season and a half or so. . . . The goals he scored and set up in 2000 and 2001 propelled the United States to four victories in the early part of the World Cup qualification process. . . . This year, he returned from the injury and performed brilliantly in several World Cup tuneup games, showcasing not only his magic with the ball but also his fiery temperament and, as important to soccer stardom as anything, his charismatic ability to entertain the crowd." That view was echoed by Giorgio Chinaglia, a leading scorer in the 1970s and 1980s on an Italian premier team and also a member of the New York Cosmos. "Clint Mathis is hungry, he's greedy, and he has a certain selfishness—all the strikers, we have this knack," Chinaglia says. "He's for real, the type of player the U.S. has never had before. He wants the ball, he demands that his teammates provide for him the ball, and when he gets it, he does things no one can imagine him doing. This is a rare skill. He'll go far, because all the teams in Europe, they're looking for someone who can score."

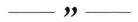

> "Clint Mathis is hungry, he's greedy, and he has a certain selfishness — all the strikers, we have this knack," said Giorgio Chinaglia, a leading scorer in the 1970s and 1980s on an Italian premier team and a former member of the New York Cosmos. "He's for real, the type of player the U.S. has never had before. He wants the ball, he demands that his teammates provide for him the ball, and when he gets it, he does things no one can imagine him doing. This is a rare skill. He'll go far, because all the teams in Europe, they're looking for someone who can score."

The 2002 World Cup

By the time Mathis returned to play, the National Team was gearing up for the 2002 World Cup. In the first qualifying round, the U.S. played against Portugal, South Korea, and Poland. Mathis wanted to play, but National Team coach Bruce Arena didn't feel he was in good enough condition to do so at first. In fact, Arena benched him during the first qualifying game against Portugal, which the American team ended up winning with a score of 3-2. The coach criticized Mathis's trash talk to opponents and his confrontational approach to referees, with resulting yellow cards. He also accused him of partying too much and not working hard enough to get into playing shape. "I'm not too worried about the trash talk, because no one playing for Portugal or South Korea or Poland is going to understand him

The United States National World Cup Soccer Team, 2002.

anyhow," Arena said. "I'm not too worried about the [yellow] cards, because that just shows his competitiveness. I am worried about his work ethic. It took him nearly seven months to heal from ACL surgery. Other players have done it in nine weeks. The greatest players work the hardest. He's going to have to learn that if he wants to play for a big club." Mathis responded by saying, "I definitely don't think that's the case. I work hard, just like everybody else, in order to enjoy my life and do the things I enjoy. If I continue to do my job on the field . . . I don't think it's anybody's business what I do off the field, as long as I get the job done."

Fans were surprised by Mathis's reduced playing time in the early World Cup games, but when he did play his contributions were significant. In a shootout against Canada, it was his successful penalty kick that put the U.S. team into the finals; he scored twice in the 4-0 victory over Honduras, and had an assist in the 1-0 victory over Ecuador. The German team, however, proved too much for the U.S. Even though Mathis scored twice, his team lost 4-2. They also lost to Ireland and the Netherlands, but won against Uruguay, Jamaica, and Portugal. A score by Mathis late in the game brought a 1-1 tie against the South Koreans in June, followed by a loss against Poland and a win over Mexico. Meeting the Germans again on June 21 in the quarterfinals, the Americans were defeated 1-0 when Michael Ballack butted the ball into the net with his head. The Americans went home without the cup, but they still had done better than any other U.S. men's team. A good deal of the credit went to Mathis.

Disappointment . . . and Hopes for the Future

Controversy and a disappointing scoring season plagued Mathis in 2002. His coaches complained about his outrageous Mohawk haircut. He hurt his right knee in July, had knee surgery, and spent some time in recovery. He missed several games before returning in mid-August and scored only four goals with the MetroStars during the year. About his weak 2002 season with the MetroStars, he commented, "I can't pinpoint it. I got mentally drained, got away from what I needed to do. I was disappointed. I was so tired. I took it out on the referees. That's just not me." Coach Octavio Zambrano felt that his temper on the field was getting out of control. There was an incident in which Mathis stepped on an opposing player—something he said was an accident—and received a major penalty. Afterwards, Zambrano even told the media that he thought Mathis could use some psychological therapy. Mathis disagreed, telling newspapers that "Octavio believes there is a problem there and the only reason he is bringing it up publicly is to get my attention. That's fine. We'll do whatever we have to do to fix it."

———— " ————

"As much as I love soccer and I wouldn't want to be doing anything else," Mathis said, "I have to look at it as a business, too. I have to look at what will benefit me and my future family down the road if I get hurt. So maybe I have to look at leaving down the road. I mean, I'd love to stay here and help soccer grow. Being an American, I would love to see my kids and grandkids playing in a soccer league based here which is run very well like they are in Europe. I'll try to do whatever is in my power to help the league grow, but at the same time, I'm realistic."

———— " ————

With his contract for the MetroStars running out in 2003, Mathis is seriously considering going to an overseas team. He has already traveled to Germany to talk with the Bayern team there. "As much as I love soccer and I wouldn't want to be doing anything else," he said, "I have to look at it as a business, too. I have to look at what will benefit me and my future family down the road if I get hurt. So maybe I have to look at leaving down the

115

Mathis celebrates after he scored the 1-0 goal during the
U.S. World Cup match against South Korea, June 2002.

road. I mean, I'd love to stay here and help soccer grow. Being an American, I would love to see my kids and grandkids playing in a soccer league based here which is run very well like they are in Europe. I'll try to do whatever is in my power to help the league grow, but at the same time, I'm realistic."

HOME AND FAMILY

Mathis is currently single and lives in a new townhouse in New Jersey. When Mathis isn't training or playing soccer, his favorite thing to do is to hang out with his friends in his basement. He remodeled his basement in 2001 when he was recovering from knee surgery. It includes a large-screen television, a pool table, and a 12-foot-long couch. "This is my pride and joy," said Mathis, who added, "My idea of an ideal Saturday night is hanging out here with friends, watching movies, playing pool." He is also involved in some charitable work, serving in 2001 as the national spokesman for the MLS New York Life Dribble, Pass, and Shoot, a national youth skills competition for kids ages six to 14.

HONORS AND AWARDS

High School Player of the Year (*Atlanta Journal-Constitution*): 1993
Gatorade Player of the Year in Georgia: 1993
First Team All-American: 1995
Third Team All-American: 1997
Goal of the Year Award (Major League Soccer): 2000
Budweiser Scoring Championship (MetroStars): 2000, 2001

FURTHER READING

Periodicals

Los Angeles Times, May 12, 2002, Part 4, p.3
New York Times, May 28, 2001, section D, p.4; Dec. 18, 2001, p.S6; May 12, 2002, p.L1
New York Times Magazine, May 26, 2002, p.40
Soccer Digest, October 2000, p.26; Feb.-Mar. 2002, p.16; June-July 2002, p.14
Sports Illustrated, May 14, 2001, p.R4; May 27, 2002, p.60; Feb. 17, 2003, p.R2
Times (London), June 5, 2002, p.2

ADDRESS

Clint Mathis
MetroStars
One Harmon Plaza, 3rd Floor
Secaucus, NJ 07094

WORLD WIDE WEB SITES

http://www.metrostars.com
http://www.mlsnet.com
http://www.ussoccer.com
http://www.ussoccerplayers.com

Donovan McNabb 1976-

American Professional Football Player with the
Philadelphia Eagles
Considered One of the Top Quarterbacks in the NFL

BIRTH

Donovan Jamal McNabb was born on November 25, 1976, in
Chicago, Illinois. His father, Samuel, is an electrical engineer
who works for the power company. His mother, Wilma, is a
registered nurse. Donovan has one brother, Sean, who is four
years older.

YOUTH

Until Donovan was eight years old, the McNabb family lived on Chicago's South Side — an area that has experienced problems with drugs and crime. Then they moved half an hour away to the quiet, middle-class suburb of Dolton, Illinois. The McNabbs were the first African-American family to move into their new neighborhood. Although many people were friendly and welcoming toward them, a few people were prejudiced against them because of their race. Before they moved into their new house, some vandals spray-painted nasty messages on it and smashed the windows. But the situation improved quickly once the McNabbs settled into their new home. Donovan, in particular, had an easy time adapting to the all-white neighborhood. He was a bright, funny child who soon attracted a wide circle of friends.

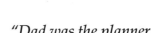

"Dad was the planner, the work-ethic guy, and the critic," McNabb noted. "Mom was the soother, the one who always kept the jokes cracking. I guess you can see those two sides from each of them in me."

Donovan grew up as part of a close-knit family that taught him the value of discipline and hard work. "You cannot be successful unless you have discipline in your life," his father stated. "What I tried to convey to both sons is that you have to be willing to work hard in life. Nothing comes easy." Although Donovan took his father's message to heart, he also developed a mischievous sense of humor as a boy. In fact, his mother always thought that he would become a comedian when he grew up. "Dad was the planner, the work-ethic guy, and the critic," Donovan noted. "Mom was the soother, the one who always kept the jokes cracking. I guess you can see those two sides from each of them in me."

Donovan loved sports as a child and covered the walls of his bedroom with pictures of professional athletes. But the person he admired most was his older brother, who was an outstanding young football player. When Donovan reached the seventh grade, he decided that he wanted to follow in Sean's footsteps and join the middle-school football team. But his mother told him he was too skinny and refused to let him play. Luckily, the coach recognized Donovan's talent and convinced his mother that he would not get hurt. Donovan played quarterback and quickly learned to avoid being hit by bigger, older boys. "At that age, you try to use a lot of juke moves because you don't want to be hit as a young child, playing football for the first time," he explained. "You watched so many big hits on TV, you don't want to be one of them. You make a lot of moves and see if you can avoid some people. Try to limit it to as few hits as you can."

EDUCATION

McNabb attended Mt. Carmel High School in Chicago—a private, all-boys' Catholic school with a reputation for both academic and athletic excellence. During his first two years of high school, it took him an hour to get to school on public transit. Once he learned to drive, however, his commute to school was cut to a half-hour. McNabb was a very good student whose favorite subject was math. But his sense of humor also came through, and he was known among his fellow students as a class clown.

———— " ————

In high school, McNabb enjoyed playing both basketball and football. "They're both fun," he said at the time. "When you're playing one, it takes your mind off the other. I don't know which sport I'm going to play in college. Right now I want to see what I can do at both sports."

———— " ————

McNabb was an outstanding athlete at Mt. Carmel. He played point guard on the varsity basketball team and was a strong defender. After leading the team to a 25-4 record during his senior season, he was named to the all-area team by the Chicago press. McNabb was also a star on the football field. As a sophomore, he played quarterback on the scout team offense that helped the starting defense prepare for that week's opponent. The defense usually preferred to play against real teams, however, because McNabb was so hard to catch. He became Mt. Carmel's starting quarterback as a junior and helped the team average over 35 points per game during the 1992 season.

McNabb enjoyed playing both basketball and football. "They're both fun," he said at the time. "When you're playing one, it takes your mind off the other. I don't know which sport I'm going to play in college. Right now I want to see what I can do at both sports." Throughout his high school career, Wilma McNabb would pay her son $10 for every touchdown he scored. Though she paid out a lot of money during football season, she always made it back during basketball season by charging him $1 for every free throw he missed.

By his senior year, McNabb had attracted the attention of college scouts across the country. Several large schools recruited him to play football. He eventually chose to attend Syracuse University in New York. Syracuse had a solid football program under Head Coach Paul Pasqualoni. In addition, Pasqualoni agreed to let the young quarterback try out for the university's powerful basketball team. Another factor in McNabb's decision was that Syracuse had a strong communications program that had produced many well-known broadcast journalists, including Bob Costas. If he was unable to make a career for himself as a professional athlete, McNabb planned to become a sportscaster. He graduated from Mt. Carmel in the spring of 1994 and entered Syracuse that fall. He earned his bachelor's degree in speech communications from the university in December 1998.

CAREER HIGHLIGHTS

College — The Syracuse University Orangemen

But of course the whole time he was at Syracuse he was also playing football. McNabb was "redshirted" during the 1994 football season, meaning that he practiced with the team but did not appear in any games. According to college athletic rules, athletes are eligible to play a sport for up to four years. Major college football programs often redshirt promising athletes during their freshmen year to give them time to adjust to the college game while retaining their full four years of eligibility. This decision paid off with McNabb, who was ready to become the starting quarterback for the Syracuse University Orangemen in the 1995 season. He led the team to a 9-2 record and was named Big East Conference Rookie of the Year. Although Syracuse lost the conference championship game to the Miami Hurricanes, they still appeared in the Gator Bowl, where they defeated the Clemson Tigers by a score of 41-0.

McNabb's parents traveled ten hours by train from Chicago to attend every Syracuse home game. They also kept in close touch with their son by telephone to make sure that he did not let his success as a big-time college quarterback change him. "I would call him periodically just to see where he was," his father recalled. "I wanted to make sure that I didn't have to come over there to Syracuse and start bursting egos. Fortunately, I didn't have to do that. He was very focused on what he wanted to do."

Immediately after the 1995 football season ended, McNabb joined the Syracuse men's basketball team. Although he spent most of his time on the bench, he still accompanied the team to the NCAA Finals, where they lost to Kentucky. McNabb's success on the football field continued during

Quarterback McNabb of the Syracuse Orangemen drops back to pass during a game against the Pittsburgh Panthers, November 1995.

the 1996 season. The sophomore quarterback led his team to a 9-3 record and a share of the Big East Championship, then helped the Orangemen defeat Houston in the Liberty Bowl. At the end of the season, McNabb was named Big East Player of the Year. He continued to be a dual-sport athlete by playing basketball again in 1996-97, but after spending another season on the bench he decided to concentrate on football.

During the 1997 football season, McNabb set a new school record with 2,892 yards in total offense. Syracuse beat Miami to win the Big East Conference, but then lost to Kansas State in the Fiesta Bowl. McNabb received Big East Player of the Year honors a second time for his performance as a junior. Syracuse had an up-and-down year in 1998, losing three straight games before turning it around. One of the highlights of Mc-Nabb's senior season came before the final home game against Miami, when he received a long, loud standing ovation from the crowd. "To be received the way I was, that was something special for myself and my parents," he stated. "That was a memorable event. It's second to none. It's something that I never expected to happen."

Syracuse went on to beat Miami 66-13 — thus handing its bitter rival its worst loss in 50 years — to win the Big East title. McNabb rushed for three touchdowns and passed for two more during the game. The Orangemen's victory over the Hurricanes earned them a trip to the Orange Bowl, where they lost to Florida in McNabb's final college game. The quarterback was named Big East Player of the Year for an unprecedented third time at the conclusion of the season.

One of the highlights of McNabb's senior season came before the final home game, when he received a long, loud standing ovation from the crowd. "To be received the way I was, that was something special for myself and my parents," he stated. "That was a memorable event. It's second to none. It's something that I never expected to happen."

McNabb left Syracuse as one of the most decorated athletes in school history. McNabb led the Orangemen to a 33-12 record in his four years as a starting quarterback. He set school records with 8,389 yards passing and 9,950 yards total offense in his career. He also established a Big East record for career touchdown passes with 77.

McNabb also earned the respect of his coaches and his fellow players with his dedication, hard work, and positive attitude. "I think he fits into the history of our program as one of the all-time great players at Syracuse," said Coach Paul Pasqualoni. "I think he fits into that from a character standpoint in the mold of unbelievable kids. He is as well-loved in the community as he is as a player. He's been perfect. He's been a role model for every kid in New York and a tremendous representative of Syracuse and a tremendous representative of Division I college football in the 1990s. The guy came in humble. He does not have a selfish bone in his body."

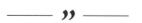

"I think he fits into the history of our program as one of the all-time great players at Syracuse," said Coach Paul Pasqualoni. *"I think he fits into that from a character standpoint in the mold of unbelievable kids. He is as well-loved in the community as he is as a player. He's been perfect. He's been a role model for every kid in New York and a tremendous representative of Syracuse and a tremendous representative of Division I college football in the 1990s. The guy came in humble. He does not have a selfish bone in his body."*

NFL — The Philadelphia Eagles

McNabb's fine college football career attracted the attention of coaches and scouts from the National Football League (NFL). It soon became clear that he would be among the players selected in the first round of the 1999 NFL draft. But his draft position was unclear, since a number of promising young quarterbacks were turning pro that year. Most football analysts appreciated McNabb's strong arm and athletic ability, but a few questioned whether he would be able to direct a complicated, pro-style offense.

In the weeks leading up to the draft, McNabb underwent interviews and workouts with several of the teams that held high draft picks. The Philadelphia Eagles — one of the worst teams in the NFL with a 3-13 record in 1998 — held the second overall pick in the draft. McNabb visited Philadelphia and impressed the Eagles coaching staff with his work ethic, leadership skills, and knowledge of the game. During one part of the interview process, quarterbacks coach Brad Childress tried to confuse McNabb by firing questions at him and forcing him to make quick decisions. "Brad was just spitting things at him, and Donovan was answering at a rapid-fire pace," Eagles Head Coach Andy Reid recalled. "Finally Brad was like, 'Slow down, would you? I can't keep up.' But that's how Donovan's mind works. He's incredibly sharp."

By the time McNabb left Philadelphia, the Eagles were certain that they had found the player they wanted to draft. Unfortunately, some Philadelphia fans had other ideas. They hoped that the Eagles would draft Ricky Williams, a powerful running back who had just won the Heisman Trophy as the best player in college football. In fact, Philadelphia Mayor Ed Rendell sponsored a city council resolution urging the team to draft Williams.

On draft day, the Cleveland Browns selected Kentucky quarterback Tim Couch with the first overall pick. The Eagles followed and selected McNabb, making him the highest-drafted African-American quarterback in NFL history. The Philadelphia fans in the audience, many of whom wore Ricky Williams jerseys, were disappointed and booed loudly when McNabb's name was announced. But McNabb took the fans' reaction in stride. He walked up to the podium and smiled, then set out to prove all the doubters wrong. "Fans are always going to state their opinion, and I respect them for that," he said. "I've learned it doesn't matter what fans say in the beginning, just as long as they are cheering in the end."

The negative reaction McNabb received on draft day bothered his friends and family members more than it bothered him. His father compared it to the situation the family faced when they moved to an all-white suburb. "What we learned from our move to Dolton is that not everyone will be happy for you when you make a success of your life," Samuel McNabb stated. "I'm constantly reminding Donovan that although he's enjoyed great popularity, not everyone's happy for him. They'll boo him again if given the chance, and they'll say ugly things about him. What's important to understand is that it's going to happen and not to let it rattle you or stop you from being the person you are."

Other McNabb supporters claimed that it was only a matter of time before Eagles fans recognized what a great choice the team had made. "They don't know it yet, but they're going to love him in Philadelphia," said Syracuse Coach Paul Pasqualoni. "It's a great marriage. In that city, with that offense, if they just give him a chance, they'll find out what a special player they've got."

Even before the football season began, McNabb began winning over the people of Philadelphia with his charm and sense of humor. For example, he appeared at a public reception and received a gift from Mayor Ed Rendell. McNabb responded by giving the major a special Eagles jersey that had McNabb's number 5 on one side, and Ricky Williams' number 34 on the other. After lengthy contract negotiations, McNabb signed a seven-year contract worth $54 million. The contract made him the highest-paid player in Eagles history and one of the highest-paid in the NFL. "I'm excit-

Philadelphia Eagles quarterback McNabb (#5) runs with the ball against the New York Giants, September 2000.

ed," McNabb noted. "I'm pretty anxious to get started. This is another step toward fulfilling my goals."

Learning the Pro Game

When McNabb joined the Eagles, the team was coming off a disastrous season in which they had ranked last in the NFL in many offensive categories. But they had recently hired a new head coach, Andy Reid, who put many new strategies in place. Reid decided to bring his rookie quarterback along slowly to help ease his adjustment to the pro game. McNabb thus began the 1999 season as the Eagles' backup quarterback. "It was frustrating at times," he admitted. "Early on, I felt I should have been in there, but I never went up to Andy and said, 'Am I going to play this week?' or 'How much am I going to play?' And you know, I didn't know what I know now. I definitely didn't grasp the magnitude of the game early on."

McNabb made his first NFL appearance during the second half of a September 19 game against the Tampa Bay Buccaneers. He was sacked six times by the tough Bucs defense. McNabb's first starting assignment did not come until November 14 against the Washington Redskins. At this point the Eagles had a 2-7 record and looked like they were headed for another disappointing season. But McNabb gave the Philadelphia fans some hope for the future by running for 49 yards, passing for another 60 yards, and leading the Eagles to a 35-28 victory.

"It was frustrating at times," McNabb said about playing backup during his first season with the Eagles. "Early on, I felt I should have been in there, but I never went up to Andy and said, 'Am I going to play this week?' or 'How much am I going to play?' And you know, I didn't know what I know now. I definitely didn't grasp the magnitude of the game early on."

The rookie quarterback kept his starting job for the rest of the season. McNabb threw his first NFL touchdown pass the following week against the Indianapolis Colts, but he also committed six turnovers in a 44-17 loss. "Things are a little faster than college," McNabb admitted. "But the biggest thing is that you have to eliminate the mistakes. You have to take care of the little things." He ended the year with 948 yards passing for 8 touchdowns, and 313 yards rushing. Although the Eagles were still bad, they had managed to win five games — three of them with McNabb as the starting quarterback. The fans had reason to be optimistic about the team's prospects for the following year, especially when the Eagles picked up several good players in the college draft and the free-agent market.

McNabb worked hard to improve his skills and conditioning during the off-season. In fact, he spent much of the summer at an elite training facility for college and professional athletes in Phoenix, Arizona. His trainers put him through such unusual drills as throwing footballs from a balance beam to improve his coordination, playing with blinders on to improve his peripheral vision, and chasing balls designed to bounce unpredictably to improve his quickness. "I was a guy coming into my second year who sat out as a rookie for most of the season and I knew I was going to start and I had to improve myself," he explained. "It was really important to get better. They paid a lot of attention to detail, to my drops, to my fundamentals, to my conditioning. . . . I left there a lot better in everything than when I started."

Making the Playoffs

McNabb entered the 2000 season as the Eagles' starting quarterback and soon became one of the NFL's rising stars. Thanks to his unique style — which combined traditional drop-back passing, passing on the run, and running with the ball — McNabb was sometimes referred to as the "quarterback of the future." He started all 16 games in his second year as a pro. He finished the season with an impressive 3,365 passing yards for 21 touchdowns and 13 interceptions. He added an amazing 629 rushing yards — an average of nearly 40 yards per game — which was the fourth-highest total for a quarterback in NFL history. With 4,000 total offensive yards, McNabb accounted for nearly 75 percent of Philadelphia's yards from scrimmage over the course of the season.

For McNabb, the most important statistic was the Eagles' 11-5 record. The team won more games than in the previous two years combined and earned a spot in the NFL playoffs. They won in the first round but were defeated in the second round by the New York Giants. Nevertheless, Philadelphia fans were thrilled with the team's quick turnaround and excited about their hot young quarterback. McNabb's performance helped him finish second in the voting for the NFL's Most Valuable Player to running back Marshall Faulk of the St. Louis Rams.

McNabb had another great year in 2000. He again started all 16 games, during which he completed 285 of 493 passes for 3,233 yards and 25 touchdowns, with 12 interceptions. He also added 482 yards rushing for 2 more touchdowns. The Eagles started the season slowly but won eight straight games at the end to earn their first division championship since 1988. They defeated Tampa Bay in the first round of the playoffs, 31-9, but then lost in the second round to the eventual Super Bowl champion Rams, 29-24. "We had a long run. We had a great run," McNabb said afterward. "We're looking forward to what we can do next year."

Before the 2002 season began, McNabb signed a 12-year, $115 million contract with the Eagles. The contract made him the highest-paid player in

NFL history and virtually guaranteed that he would play out the rest of his career in Philadelphia. "It means a lot," he noted. "You see players who were great players and Hall of Fame players who just didn't stay with their given team. To know that I'll be locked into the Philly area is a wonderful feeling for me and for my family."

Injury Threatens Playoff Run

The Eagles started out well in the 2002 season, posting a 6-3 record. But then an injury to their star quarterback threatened to keep the team out of the playoffs. McNabb suffered a broken fibula—the outside bone in the ankle—on November 17 during the third play of the Eagles' game against the Arizona Cardinals. He left the game for a few plays but then returned to action, not realizing that his ankle was broken. "I've always said that you have to put everything on the line," he explained. "That's the only way you get trust from your teammates. That's what I did. I didn't know the ankle was broken because I'd never broken anything in my life. I thought it was a high ankle sprain. I wasn't going to take myself out of the game because of a nagging injury. I had worked too hard in the off-season and set my goals too high to take myself out of a game for something I thought was little."

> "I've always said that you have to put everything on the line," McNabb explained. "That's the only way you get trust from your teammates. That's what I did. I didn't know the ankle was broken because I'd never broken anything in my life. I thought it was a high ankle sprain. I wasn't going to take myself out of the game because of a nagging injury. I had worked too hard in the off-season and set my goals too high to take myself out of a game for something I thought was little."

Although McNabb was limping noticeably, he still managed to complete 20 of 25 passes for 255 yards and four touchdowns. His outstanding performance lifted the Eagles to a 38-17 victory. However, the game marked the first time in his career that he did not have a rushing attempt. Once the game ended, McNabb submitted to an X-ray and learned the truth about his injury. The broken ankle forced him to the bench after 10 games. By this point in the season, McNabb had already completed 211 of 361 passes for 2,289 yards and 17 touchdowns, with only 6 interceptions. He had also added 460 yards rushing for 6 touchdowns.

Philadelphia Eagles quarterback McNabb looks for an open man during this divisional playoff game against the Atlanta Falcons, January 2003.

McNabb ended up spending the next six weeks watching from the sidelines. "I saw the game from a different perspective. I learned things," he recalled. "I got my pen and paper out and wrote down some things I thought would help me out." To the surprise of many fans, the Eagles won five of their next six games under the guidance of veteran backup quarterbacks Koy Detmer and A.J. Feeley.

Philadelphia claimed the top playoff seed in the National Football Conference, which earned them a bye in the first round. This gave McNabb an extra week to recover from his injury and get ready to return to the starting lineup. "It takes an entire team to win, and that's what we've done," he stated. "I couldn't be more proud of the way the guys played with me on the sidelines. I'm excited for what the team accomplished and I'm excited about returning for the playoffs."

McNabb started at quarterback on January 11 during the Eagles' playoff game against the Atlanta Falcons. Though he looked a little rusty at times, he completed 20 of 30 passes for 247 yards and also ran four times for 24 yards to lead his team to a 20-6 victory. The following week the Eagles played against the Tampa Bay Buccaneers for the right to represent the NFC in the Super Bowl. Unfortunately, Tampa's attacking defense proved too much for McNabb, who looked tentative throughout the game. Although he completed 26 of 49 passes for 243 yards, and added 17 yards rushing, most of these yards came when the result of the game was no longer in doubt. McNabb also fumbled the ball twice and threw an interception that led to a key Buccaneer touchdown. The Eagles lost 27-10 in their last home game at historic Veterans Stadium.

> *McNabb accepted full responsibility for the team's failure to reach the Super Bowl. "I played poorly. No reason. I just played poorly. It all starts with the quarterback. I had the opportunity to make plays. And, being the leader of the team, I had to make them. It happens. You want [the game] back, but there's nothing you can do. All you can do is put it behind you and live your life. I'm going to use this as motivation in the off-season."*

McNabb accepted full responsibility for the team's failure to reach the Super Bowl. "I played poorly. No reason. I just played poorly. It all starts with the quarterback. I had the opportunity to make plays. And, being the leader of the team, I had to make them," he acknowledged. "It happens.

You want [the game] back, but there's nothing you can do. All you can do is put it behind you and live your life. I'm going to use this as motivation in the off-season."

Quarterback of the Future

With his strong arm and great running ability, McNabb is often considered to be at the forefront of a new generation of athletic quarterbacks. He has enhanced his natural talents and earned the respect of his teammates and coaches with hard work and dedication to the game of football. He arrives at the Eagles practice facility at 6:30 every morning, spends the whole day working out, practicing with the team, meeting with the coaches, and studying game films, and finally returns home at 6:30 at night. McNabb recognizes that his position as quarterback makes him a leader on his team, so he tries to set a good example for his fellow players. "When you go in the huddle and you go up to the line of scrimmage, you have to look guys in the eye," he stated. "And, once you look them in the eye, and they can see how serious you are about the game, how much you love the game, then it'll rub off on some other players."

"My dad told me something when I was younger that I'll never forget. He said there will always be somebody out there who's better than I am, and the only way I'll beat this guy is to outwork him. I believe that. I can't let up because right now someone is out there studying film, lifting weights, and running and throwing passes. He wants to be better so that he can help his team win. I can see this guy. I always keep him in mind. . . ."

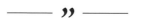

Even though he works hard and takes the game seriously, McNabb has maintained his sense of humor over the years. In fact, he is regarded as one of the funniest and best-liked players in the Eagles' locker room. McNabb is particularly known for his impersonations of the Philadelphia coaches and his fellow players. When he pretends to be Head Coach Andy Reid, he pulls his shorts up until the waistband reaches his chest and then stomps around the locker room. "I walked in on a team meeting, and Donovan was up at the front, talking and acting like me," Reid recalled. "The whole team was cracking up. He had imitated every coach—a whole stand-up comedy routine."

McNabb is not satisfied with his current level of success. He plans to continue striving to be the best player he can be and ultimately lead his team to the Super Bowl. "It's not time to relax yet," he stated. "My dad told me something when I was younger that I'll never forget. He said there will always be somebody out there who's better than I am, and the only way I'll beat this guy is to outwork him. I believe that. I can't let up because right now someone is out there studying film, lifting weights, and running and throwing passes. He wants to be better so that he can help his team win. I can see this guy. I always keep him in mind. . . . I play this game to be the best. And the only sure way I know to be the best is to outwork everybody else. Some people take one step toward their dream, accomplish a little something, and then feel like that's it. Not me. I'm never satisfied."

> "

> "*. . . I play this game to be the best. And the only sure way I know to be the best is to outwork everybody else. Some people take one step toward their dream, accomplish a little something, and then feel like that's it. Not me. I'm never satisfied.*"

> "

HOME AND FAMILY

McNabb lives in Cherry Hill, New Jersey—a suburb of Philadelphia—in a house he shares with his older brother and his two dogs, a boxer named Sinbad and a Rottweiler named Diego. In May 2002 he became engaged to his longtime girlfriend, Raquel Nurse (known as Roxi). The couple met during their freshman year of college. Nurse was a star guard on the Syracuse women's basketball team. In fact, she still holds the school record for career assists with 530, and she was named Big East Conference scholar-athlete of the year for 1997-98. McNabb proposed marriage while they were together on a vacation cruise. "My girlfriend's been there for me when things were pretty tough, and there when they were going well," he explained. "She's been there when I wasn't the Donovan McNabb everyone in Philly knows about, when I was a rinky-dink kid in college trying to win a starting job on the football team."

McNabb remains close to his parents, who still travel from Chicago to attend many of his home games. The fact that McNabb is wealthy and famous makes no difference in the way his parents treat him. In fact, his mother still calls to scold him if she sees a picture of him on TV or in a magazine wearing pants that need to be pulled up. "My mother and father have always been there for me, in anything I do . . . to make me a better person," McNabb stated. "That's where it all starts. They gave me guidance and advice, whether I asked for it or not. They've been my number one fans, and my number one critics."

HOBBIES AND OTHER INTERESTS

McNabb tries to lead a normal life outside of football. He enjoys relaxing with friends, playing video games, watching movies, and attending Philadelphia 76ers basketball games. "I do the same things everybody else does. It's just you might see me on Sunday playing football," he said. "People say, 'He's in the NFL, his head's going to blow up. He's a young guy. He doesn't know what he has.' Man, I know what I have. It's just that I don't show people. I just take things in stride, know what I'm saying? You won't see me in flashy cars or flashy clothes. That's just me."

> "My mother and father have always been there for me, in anything I do . . . to make me a better person," McNabb stated. "That's where it all starts. They gave me guidance and advice, whether I asked for it or not. They've been my number one fans, and my number one critics."

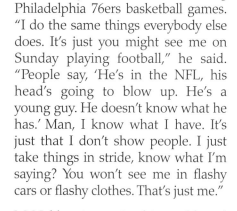

McNabb enjoys using his wealth and fame to help others. For example, he donated $100,000 to help renovate the football locker room at Syracuse University. "I am delighted to pay back, in some small way, all that I have gained from having graduated from Syracuse University and for having been a part of the great Syracuse football tradition," he said of the gift. "It's just a little appreciation for everything that they've done throughout my college career." In 2002 the university invited McNabb to become the youngest member on its board of trustees. McNabb has also donated money for scholarships to help deserving students attend Mt. Carmel High School.

The cause that is closest to McNabb's heart is the fight against diabetes. Diabetes is a disease in which the body does not produce or properly use insulin, a chemical that aids in the digestion of sugar. It is a serious, chronic condition that has no cure. The disease often causes complications such as blindness, heart disease, and kidney failure. Diabetes affects over 15 million people in the United States and is the nation's seventh-leading cause of death. McNabb's grandmother died from diabetes, and his father has been diagnosed with the disease. "My father Samuel was diagnosed with Type 2 diabetes five years ago," he noted. "What both of us learned along the way motivated us to help people avoid or minimize the consequences of this terrible disease."

McNabb serves as a national spokesperson for the American Diabetes Association. He also sponsors an all-star weekend each year to raise money for diabetes research. The event includes a football clinic with several big-name NFL players, a gala awards dinner, a prayer brunch, and a celebrity all-star basketball game. Finally, McNabb is active in charitable events in the Philadelphia area. For example, every year at Christmastime he dresses up as Santa Claus and distributes gifts to needy children at a local community center. In addition to his charity work, McNabb also does a lot of paid endorsements. One of his favorites is a humorous commercial for Campbell's Chunky Soup that also features his mother.

HONORS AND AWARDS

Big East Conference Rookie of the Year: 1995
First Team All-Big East Conference Quarterback: 1995, 1996, 1997, 1998
Big East Conference Offensive Player of the Year: 1996, 1997, 1998
Gator Bowl Most Valuable Player: 1996
Big East Conference Player of the Year (*Football News*): 1998
Big East Conference Player of the Decade: 1990s
NFL Player of the Year (CBS Radio): 2000
Offensive Most Valuable Player (Philadelphia Eagles): 2000
Terry Bradshaw Award (Fox Sports): 2000
NFL Pro Bowl: 2000, 2001, 2002
Wanamaker Award (City of Philadelphia): 2002

FURTHER READING

Books

Contemporary Black Biography, Vol. 29, 2001
Who's Who among African Americans, 2002

Periodicals

Chicago Sun-Times, July 21, 1992, p.74
Fort Lauderdale Sun-Sentinel, Dec. 29, 1998, p.C8
New York Times, Aug. 25, 1996, Sec. 8, p.7
Philadelphia Daily News, Sep. 6, 2001, p.E3; Jan. 18, 2002, p.E8; May 18, 2002, Sec. Local, p.3; Jan. 13, 2003, Sec. Sports, p.120; Jan. 20, 2003, Sports sec., p.134

Philadelphia Inquirer, July 22, 1999, p.D1; July 31, 1999, p.C1; Dec. 5, 1999, p.A1; Jan. 18, 2002, p.E4; Sep. 28, 2002, p.D1; Nov. 18, 2002, p.A1; Jan. 13, 2003, p.D6; Jan. 18, 2003, p.D1; Jan. 20, 2003, p.E14; Jan. 22, 2003, p.D7
Sporting News, Apr. 20, 1998, p.59; Dec. 18, 2000, p.18; June 18, 2001, p.52
Sports Illustrated, Aug. 1, 1996, p.50; May 17, 1999, p.38; July 30, 2001, p.58; Jan. 28, 2002, p.38; Jan. 20, 2003, p.44; Jan. 27, 2003, p.48
Sports Illustrated for Kids, Sep. 1, 2001, p.41
St. Louis Post-Dispatch, Sep. 9, 2001, p.E1
USA Today, Jan. 20, 2003, p.C6

Online Articles

http://www.phillyhealthandfitness.com/Interviews/McNabb.htm
    (*Philly Health and Fitness,* "The Sorcery behind the Spiral: McNabbracadabra!" Dec. 2, 2002)
http://www.superbowl.com/insider/story/6111179
    (*NFL Insider,* "McNabb: If I Have to Run, I'll Run," Jan. 7, 2003)

Online Database

Biography Resource Center Online, 2003, article from *Contemporary Black Biography,* 2001

ADDRESS

Donovan McNabb
Philadelphia Eagles
One Navacare Way
Philadelphia, PA 19145

WORLD WIDE WEB SITES

http://www.donovanmcnabb.com
http://www.nfl.com/players/playerpage/133361
http://www.philadelphiaeagles.com/store/the_team/players.asp?id=2
http://www.jockbio.com/Bios/McNabb/McNabb_bio.html

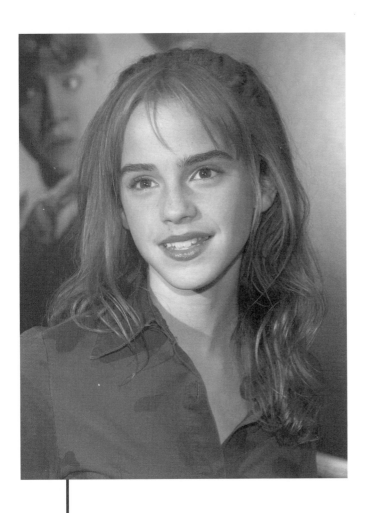

Emma Watson 1990-

British Actress
Stars as Hermione in the Hit Films *Harry Potter and the Sorcerer's Stone* and *Harry Potter and the Chamber of Secrets*

BIRTH

Emma Charlotte Duerre Watson was born on April 15, 1990, and lives in Oxford, England. Her parents, Jacqueline Watson and Chris Watson, are both lawyers and are divorced. She has one brother, Alex, who is three years younger.

YOUTH

Emma Watson grew up with a very normal childhood in Oxford, England. Oxford is a city not far from London, and it is known for its famous university. She spends time with her brother and with each of her parents. She has two cats named Bubbles and Domino. She enjoys school (except for geography and math) and likes to play sports, such as hockey, rowing, tennis, and a game called rounders, which is similar to baseball. She attends The Dragon School, a private prep school, where she has many friends. Watson has participated in several of the school's dramatic productions, playing Morgan La Fay in *Arthur: The Young Years*, the swallow in *The Swallow and the Prince*, the angry cook in *Alice in Wonderland*, and a lead role in *The Happy Prince*. She also attended classes at Stagecoach Theatre Arts, a network of performing arts schools across England.

"I just stood there staring for it seemed like five minutes. It was just too much to take in," Watson said about being offered the role of Hermione. "It was the scariest thing that ever happened to me. It was the biggest thing that ever happened to me. It was the best thing that ever happened to me. I love the idea of people liking me and seeing me as a role model. I think that is very flattering."

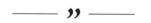

CAREER HIGHLIGHTS

Auditioning for the Role of Hermione

Watson says that she wanted to be an actress since she was three years old. She enjoyed being in school productions as she was growing up, but her big break came when moviemakers were searching all over England for the right child actors for the first Harry Potter movie. "My dad read me the first and second books, and I was in the middle of the third book when I started auditioning. I was a really big fan." Some of the auditions were held in the gym at Watson's school. The casting directors asked the school staff for the names of students who might fit the parts, and one of the teachers recommended Emma Watson. "It sounded like fun so I did it. I did the first one and got through to the second audition and that was a bit more serious because they had me on camera."

After the second audition, Watson was called to Leavesden Studios outside of London. She and Rupert Grint were called into producer David Hey-

A scene from Harry Potter and the Sorcerer's Stone, *2001.*

man's office and asked if they would like to play the parts of Hermione and Ron. "That was an amazing moment. My Dad was waiting outside. He thought it was just going to be about another audition." At first, she wasn't sure it was real. "I just stood there staring for it seemed like five minutes. It was just too much to take in." It was a turning point in Watson's life. "It was the scariest thing that ever happened to me. It was the biggest thing that ever happened to me. It was the best thing that ever happened to me. I love the idea of people liking me and seeing me as a role model. I think that is very flattering."

Harry Potter and the Sorcerer's Stone

Watson was offered the role of Hermione, one of the main characters in the Harry Potter books. Harry Potter is a young wizard, age 11 when the series begins, who doesn't know that he has magical powers. His parents died when he was a baby, and he has been living with his cruel aunt and uncle ever since. Harry's aunt and uncle have never told him that another magical world exists among the regular, non-magical "Muggle" world. After some amazing events, he comes to attend boarding school at the Hogwarts School of Witchcraft and Wizardry. He meets two other new students, Ron and Hermione, who become his closest friends. Hermione is the daughter of Muggle parents — she just happens to have magical powers. She is a very serious student who loves to learn, and she is quite determined to follow the rules and do things properly. Unfortunately, her friendship with the famous Harry Potter keeps getting her into all different kinds of trouble.

———— " ————

"I'm not obsessed with books," Watson said about how she's different from Hermione. "I'm not obsessed with school and homework, and I'm not obsessed with not getting into trouble. I'm not obsessed with woolly grandma-knitted jumpers, and I hope I've got a better sense of fashion. So no, I'm not like [Hermione]. . . ."

———— " ————

Watson started shooting *Harry Potter and the Sorcerer's Stone* soon after the offer from producer David Heyman, and her dreams of being a movie star turned into the reality of hard work. "It's definitely not what you would call glamorous. You have to wake up really early in the morning. I think the earliest they ever called me in was a six o'clock pick-up, which means you have to be in the car and leaving by six. I prefer getting up late in the morning and coming back late at night. I did enjoy it though." Acting for the movies also means doing scenes over and over and over again. "When you do a scene 20 times it can get boring. But it's mostly great because every day you are doing a different scene with different people." There is also the hard work of doing some of the stunts herself, such as in the troll scene in *Harry Potter and the Sorcerer's Stone*. "In the girls toilets, they have these six cubicles and I have to climb under them. They put a safety mat under them but that made it very hard to do. We actually measured the space and there was only 30 cms clearance. I bumped my head every time I had to duck under one. I had to crawl along the sinks dodging the troll. That was fun!"

Watson has enjoyed working with director Chris Columbus, who has helped her make an easy transition from school plays to major film productions. "[He's] really good with working with children, and he really got us into the moment, and he made us feel really, really, comfortable. He's a great director." Some of Columbus's requirements were difficult, though — like keeping the stories' secrets until the premiere. "It was hard. I was frightened that in the press conferences I was going to tell everybody that it was all fake. A lot of it had to be secret even from my family, there were things I couldn't tell my grandmother."

Although she spent months on the set of *Harry Potter and the Sorcerer's Stone*, Watson had to wait along with everyone to see the finished product at the premiere. After watching it, she found that it met her expectations perfectly. "I feel like they've kind of just like taken a piece of my mind out from the book and just used it on the film, because it is exactly as I imagined it I—I mean, I suppose every actress, when they like see themselves on screen they're like, 'Oh, they cut out my best lines,' or 'Oh, I look so bad in that scene,' or 'Oh, my hair looks disastrous.' But I think everyone says that. So I'm very self-critical, but altogether I just loved the film. It's amazing."

Harry Potter and the Chamber of Secrets

Coming back to work on the second film, *Harry Potter and the Chamber of Secrets*, was much easier for Watson. "I enjoyed making the second one much more than I did the first one. . . . [We] knew the cast, we knew the crew, we knew the director, and let's face it, we knew what we were doing the second time around, which was good. Yeah, I think it was—I also enjoyed watching the second one a lot more. I think it's much, much better than the first one." Watson, along with Rupert Grint and Daniel Radcliffe as Ron and Harry, are all scheduled to appear in the third film as well. After that, no one is certain what will happen, especially as the young actors grow and mature faster than their screen characters.

Watson likes her character Hermione, who is fun, annoying, and demanding to play. "I reckon that Hermione is pretty bossy, pretty swotty, pretty teacher's pet." Her lines give Watson a challenging time occasionally. "I think Hermione gets all of the big words to say. Some of them are a real mouthful. She gets the long sentences and long complicated words, which even I can't understand. . . . It's like tongue twisters in every paragraph. But she does get good lines. It's hard, especially when you have to do it quickly. There are always so many things going on in your mind. You try and remember your lines but it's not just that. You have to get on your mark, make sure you are in the light, that the camera can see you, making sure you are not blocking the person behind you, and then you have to remember your lines with all of that." Watson thinks that Ron gets the brunt of Hermione's "snooty" lines. Her personal favorite, though, was, "We're going to get killed, or worse, expelled!"

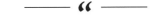

"Instead of spending my time doing academic things like she does, I do lots more sports. I play hockey, tennis, and rounders at my school. I spend a lot of time with my friends and I like being at home a lot. It must be quite hard for Hermione to be away from home at Hogwarts."

A scene from Harry Potter and the Chamber of Secrets, *2002, of Watson brewing a potion in the girls' bathroom.*

Watson seems to like some of Hermione's character traits but not others. "She's self-assured, irritating, emotional, and loyal." As she has worked on the two films, she has gotten to know Hermione's character better and has grown to like her more. "I like the way she's developing. She's more interesting to play (in the second Potter film) because she is maturing, growing up. Emotionally, she's becoming more independent. And in the second film, she's the one who gets knocked down, but I thinks she winds up on top."

Working with an all-star cast has also been exciting for an aspiring young actress. One of her favorite scenes was in the second film. "That was really good to film. That was really good. I was also kind of nervous about meeting Gilderoy Lockhart—well, actually, Kenneth Branagh, who plays Gilderoy Lockhart, obviously, because he's like such an amazing Shakespearean actor and everything. . . . He is absolutely hilarious. He is so funny. But he's also really down to earth. He's just like a really nice guy."

Combining Acting and School

During filming, Watson and the other young actors are allowed to work between three and five hours a day. When they are not doing a scene, they work with a tutor to keep up on schoolwork. "It's one to one, so even though we do, like, half the amount we would do in a normal school day, you get just as much work done because it's one to one. And when you're in a class, you know, it takes a little longer." School on a film set also has other advantages. "We don't get any homework, which is cool, and no detentions, which is even cooler." Watson enjoys her regular school and misses her friends when she isn't there. But she doesn't overdo it, like Hermione. "I'm not obsessed with

"I've been at my school for seven years so I know all my friends very, very well and I think they are just curious and interested, and otherwise they are exactly the same. I still see them. I still go to the cinema with them. It's quite hard to keep in touch with all of my friends when I'm filming but I do my best."

books. I'm not obsessed with school and homework, and I'm not obsessed with not getting into trouble. I'm not obsessed with woolly grandma-knitted jumpers, and I hope I've got a better sense of fashion. So no, I'm not like [Hermione]. Instead of spending my time doing academic things like she does, I do lots more sports. I play hockey, tennis, and rounders at my school. I spend a lot of time with my friends and I like being at home a lot. It must be quite hard for Hermione to be away from home at Hogwarts."

Watson's friendships seem to have withstood her new fame quite well. "I've been at my school for seven years so I know all my friends very, very well and I think they are just curious and interested, and otherwise they are exactly the same. I still see them. I still go to the cinema with them. It's quite hard to keep in touch with all of my friends when I'm filming but I do my best." When she is back at school full-time, though, some of the other students who she doesn't know as well aren't as calm about it. "I go to a very big school and some people give me a bit of stick. They walk past and go 'Wingardium Leviosa' for the billionth time that day, and I go aaagggghhhhh!"

> "People stop me in the street. Everywhere. And mostly, they say, 'Hi, Hermione,' and I say, 'Hi,' back. But it's scary. It's quite scary to be 10 feet tall on the screen and that everyone knows everything about you, at least physically. You are kind of being watched all the time. Most people are really nice but some stare, like you're some kind of zoo exhibit and not a real person with real feelings."

Dealing with Fame

Watson went from being a normal pre-teen to one of the most famous faces on earth after *Harry Potter and the Sorcerer's Stone* opened to huge audiences in 2001. The success of *Harry Potter and the Chamber of Secrets* in 2002 made her even more recognizable. Life in public isn't the same anymore. "People stop me in the street. Everywhere. And mostly, they say, 'Hi, Hermione,' and I say, 'Hi,' back. But it's scary. It's quite scary to be 10 feet tall on the screen and that everyone knows everything about you, at least physically. You are kind of being watched all the time. Most people are really nice but some stare, like you're some kind of zoo exhibit and not a real person with real feelings."

Fan mail is a regular part of her life now, and some of it is more than just paper or email. "When it was my birthday, someone sent me a massive white cuddly bear, almost as big as me. They sent it in the post! I just thought that was amazing, as they'd never even met me or anything."

Being part of a hugely successful movie has meant earning a lot of money, too, but Watson doesn't pay too much attention to that part of the experience. She lets her parents handle it all and doesn't even know how much she has made. She knows that it is in the bank until she is 21, and then she'll decide what to do with it.

Emma Watson (right) and Daniel Radcliffe (left) pose for photographs with J.K. Rowling at the world premiere of Harry Potter and the Chamber of Secrets, *London, November 2002.*

The amazing changes that have come about from one audition don't seem to phase Watson. Her life still seems normal to her. "You know, I still fall out with my brother, I still have to make my bed, I still see my friends, I try to lead a really normal life. Basically, the only way that it's changed is what I'm doing in everyday life."

HOBBIES AND OTHER INTERESTS

Watson insists that although she likes school and reading, she is not the bookworm that Hermione is. "And I hope I have better fashion sense." She likes to shop; her big reward for completing the first Harry Potter movie was a clothes shopping spree. Some of her favorite makers are DKNY and the Gap. "I wear a uniform at school, but I have these massive bell-bottom flares, and my mom really disapproves of them." Her favorite animals are cats, and she has two. Pop music is another interest, and some of her favorite performers are Bryan Adams, Suzanne Vega, Samantha Mumba, and Dido. Movies, of course, are of great interest to the rising actress. Some of her role models include Julia Roberts, Sandra Bullock, John Cleese, and Goldie Hawn. Watson also plays many different sports, and she hopes to get an art scholarship to college when she is 18.

MOVIES

Harry Potter and the Sorcerer's Stone, 2001
Harry Potter and the Chamber of Secrets, 2002

FURTHER READING

Periodicals

Chicago Sun-Times, Nov. 29, 2002, p.32
Daily Telegraph (London), Oct. 25, 2002, p.23
Entertainment Weekly, Dec. 21, 2001, p.52
Newsday, Nov. 8, 2002, p.D6
Los Angeles Times, Nov. 10, 2002, p.E12
Ottawa Citizen, Nov. 6, 2001, p.D9
People, Nov. 19, 2001, p.64
Toronto Sun, Nov. 10, 2002, p.S14
USA Today, Nov. 20, 2001, p.D10

Online Articles

http://news.bbc.co.uk/cbbcnews/hi/tv_film/newsid_1628000/1628670.stm
    (*BBC Newsround,* "Emma Watson: 'I Have the Best Lines,'" Oct. 30, 2001)
http://www.ew.com/ew/report/0,6115,188388~1~0~harrpottershermion
    etalks,00.html(*Entertainment Weekly,* "Season of the Witch," no date)

ADDRESS

Emma Watson
Warner Bros.
4000 Warner Boulevard
Burbank, CA 91522

WORLD WIDE WEB SITE

http://harrypotter.warnerbros.com/home.html

Reese Witherspoon 1976-

American Actress
Star of the Hit Films *Legally Blonde* and *Sweet Home Alabama*

BIRTH

Reese Witherspoon was born Laura Jean Reese Witherspoon on March 26, 1976, in New Orleans, Louisiana. Her father, John Witherspoon, is a surgeon; her mother, Betty (Reese) Witherspoon, is a nurse with a Ph.D. in pediatric nursing who teaches at the college level. She has a brother, John, Jr., who is three years older.

Witherspoon comes from a very old and distinguished family. One of her father's ancestors, John D. Witherspoon, was a Scottish immigrant who signed the Declaration of Independence and became the first president of Princeton University.

YOUTH

Witherspoon's father was a surgeon in the U.S. Air Force, so Reese spent her first five years living in Germany and traveling throughout Europe. Then her family settled in Nashville, Tennessee, where she and her brother grew up in a very stable and loving home. "I walked to school every day," she says. "My grandmother lived down the street. My grandfather grew all our vegetables in his garden." She idolized her father, who had achieved a perfect score on his S.A.T.s and graduated at the top of his class from Yale. Her mother had a number of college degrees and set high academic standards for her children.

> *"There was a little girl who lived down the street and her parents owned a flower shop, and they asked me to be in their local commercial," Witherspoon recalls. "I came home and told my mother I wanted to be an actress."*

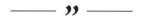

Witherspoon was barely in grade school when she became interested in acting. "There was a little girl who lived down the street and her parents owned a flower shop, and they asked me to be in their local commercial," Witherspoon recalls. "I came home and told my mother I wanted to be an actress." Her parents had hoped their daughter would follow in their footsteps and pursue a medical career, but they didn't try to stand in her way. The enrolled her in acting classes at age seven and let her start modeling for department store ads when she was 10. Within a couple of years she was appearing in TV commercials.

Becoming an Actress

When Witherspoon was 14, she heard that Robert Mulligan, who had directed *To Kill a Mockingbird,* was making a movie in the Nashville area. She auditioned for a role as an extra, but to her surprise, she was given one of the leading roles in *The Man in the Moon,* a story about a young girl growing up in the south in the 1950s. As Dani Trant, she falls in love with a 17-year-old neighbor, only to discover that he is much more interested in her older sister. *The Hollywood Reporter* called Witherspoon's performance "flawless." Although she was barely a teenager, her interest in acting suddenly seemed like more than just a hobby.

After *The Man in the Moon*, Witherspoon was offered a number of smaller television and movie roles. She appeared in "Wildflower," a 1991 HBO movie directed by the well-known actress Diane Keaton. It tells the story of a young woman in the 1930s who is partially deaf and suffers from epileptic seizures, for which her stepfather has locked her in a shed for most of her life. Witherspoon played Ellie, the tomboy who discovers this woman and decides to rescue her. The following year she played Cassie in "Desperate Choices: To Save My Child," another television drama, about a young girl suffering from leukemia who needs a bone marrow transplant. She also appeared with Danny DeVito in the film *Jack the Bear*. Then she got another starring role, this time in a Disney adventure movie called *A Far Off Place*, which was filmed in Africa's Kalahari Desert. As Nonnie, a teenage girl who has been raised in Africa and whose parents have been killed by elephant poachers, she undertakes a dangerous journey across the desert with a teenage companion named Harry (Ethan Randall), whose parents have also been murdered but who shows little understanding or appreciation of the African way of life.

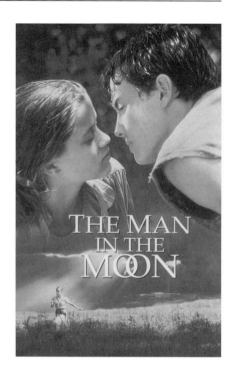

Many parents would have had reservations about letting their teenage daughter take time away from her studies or travel all the way to Africa to appear in a movie. But Witherspoon gives credit to her parents for their open-mindedness and their willingness to support their daughter's interests. "I have to say that one of the greatest things that my parents did was to encourage my individuality," she told an interviewer some years later. "They just said Okay."

After she returned from filming *A Far Off Place*, Witherspoon had a minor role as the teenage wife of a Scottish land baron in "Return to Lonesome

Dove," a sequel to the Emmy Award-winning television miniseries of the late 1980s. But the sequel was panned by TV critics for its slow pace and mediocre acting.

EDUCATION

While she was already a working actress, Witherspoon attended an elite private all-girls high school in Nashville called Harpeth Hall. She was a top student, a cheerleader, and a debutante who wore a long white gown to her "coming out" ball, a ritual that marks a young woman's introduction to polite society. But she was also what she describes as "the classic nerd who was reading books all the time." She particularly loved doing research in the library and writing papers.

> *"I wore a uniform to school, and I have to say I liked it a lot. It was good not to be so concerned about how I looked. In high school, you are so concerned about your look and your body 'cause you're changing a lot.*
> *I thought it was so cool not to have that pressure, and the comfort to be yourself. And it sucks when you can't afford things or another person doesn't like what you're wearing. That's a terrible feeling."*

When Witherspoon was a teenager, she loved to shop. But except for the Gap, there weren't a lot of good stores near her home. So she ended up buying a lot from catalogs. "I became a catalog shopper growing up and I had to order all my clothes. I would die when I got the new J. Crew catalog 'cause I wanted to have the stuff before my friends." But she couldn't wear those clothes to school at Harpeth Hall. Instead, she wore a uniform. "I wore a uniform to school, and I have to say I liked it a lot," she admits. "It was good not to be so concerned about how I looked. In high school, you are so concerned about your look and your body 'cause you're changing a lot. I thought it was so cool not to have that pressure, and the comfort to be yourself. And it sucks when you can't afford things or another person doesn't like what you're wearing. That's a terrible feeling."

Witherspoon's high school grades were good enough to get her accepted at Stanford University. But after graduating from Harpeth Hall in 1994 she took a year off to appear in a series of films that provided her with more wide-ranging acting experience. In *S.F.W.* she played a hostage trapped in a Los Angeles convenience store. The film received negative reviews, but the "gentle dignity" of Witherspoon's performance attracted notice. She won even higher praise and more public attention for her role in *Fear* as an innocent teenage girl whose relationship with a boy (Mark Wahlberg) she doesn't know very well turns violent when the girl's father tries to keep them apart. *Overnight Delivery* was a more lighthearted film in which she and Paul Rudd travel across the country trying to intercept an overnight delivery letter. Her last film during this period was *Freeway*, a retelling of "Little Red Riding Hood" in which a girl named Vanessa (Witherspoon) is on her way to visit her grandmother when she is picked up on a California highway by a serial killer named Wolverton (Keifer Sutherland). Vanessa, whose mother is a drug addict and whose boyfriend has sexually abused her, turns on her captor and shoots him—quite a change from the innocent young girls Witherspoon had been playing up to this point in her career.

When Witherspoon entered Stanford, she studied English literature and thought about going on to medical school. But after her freshman year she was given an opportunity to star in a film called *Twilight*. "I had to make a choice between Psych 101 and starring in a film opposite Paul Newman, Gene Hackman, Susan Sarandon, and James Garner," she says. "My parents didn't quite understand my decision, but to me it was a no-brainer."

CAREER HIGHLIGHTS

In *Twilight,* Witherspoon plays Mel Ames, the 17-year-old daughter of two movie stars, Jack and Catherine Ames (Gene Hackman and Susan Sarandon). When Mel runs off to be with her boyfriend, Jack and Catherine ask retired private investigator Harry Ross (Paul Newman) to find her and bring her home. Mel ends up accidentally shooting and injuring Harry, who is given a place to live on Jack and Catherine's estate. The plot is complicated by the fact that Jack is dying of cancer and Harry has a long-standing romantic interest in Catherine, whose first husband disappeared 20 years ago and is believed to have committed suicide, although the case has never been solved. It is Harry's involvement in this 20-year-old mystery that becomes the film's focus.

Witherspoon's decision to interrupt her education to appear in a film with Oscar-winning actors Newman, Hackman, and Sarandon turned out to be a smart career move. She was soon receiving so many other movie offers that returning to Stanford was out of the question.

Reese Witherspoon and Tobey Maguire in Pleasantville, 1998.

Spreading Her Wings

Witherspoon appeared in four more movies during 1998-99, playing very different roles in each and proving herself to be a talented and versatile actress. In *Pleasantville* she plays Jennifer, the teenage sister of David (Tobey Maguire), who is obsessed with a 1950s sitcom that is being re-broadcast on cable television. Jennifer and David have a tough home life, with divorced parents who always seem to be fighting with each other. So for David, the simple and secure life depicted in his favorite TV show is very appealing and comforting. One day, the two siblings get into an argument over the remote control—David wants to watch his re-runs while Jennifer wants to watch a concert on MTV. The remote breaks, and a mysterious TV repairman gives them a new high-tech remote that transports them back to the 1950s in Pleasantville, the location of David's favorite sitcom. They discover that they are now Bud and Mary Sue in a black-and-white world. In Pleasantville, the weather is always sunny and no one ever steps out of line. It's a strange world, with no toilets, no fire, no rain, and no double beds—not even for married couples. It's a completely sanitized life, one in which the other inhabitants don't seem to realize its limitations. Life is predictable, safe, and nonthreatening—but also boring, stifling, repressed, and unimaginative, with enforced conformity. There's no passion, no strong emotions. At first, Bud makes a fairly easy adjustment to his new life, but Mary Sue sets out to change it. Eventually both Bud and Mary Sue begin to affect others, and people begin to experience strange new thoughts and emotions, which are reflected in the bursts of color that begin to appear in Pleasantville's formerly black-and-white world. The movie won praise from critics as a clever, provocative, and complex parable, and Witherspoon won raves for her performance.

Cruel Intentions is a 1990s version of the 1782 French novel, *Les liaisons dangereuses* (*Dangerous Liaisons*), by Pierre Choderlos de Laclos. This novel about the corruption of innocence has been adapted for the big screen several times, including an Oscar-winning version in 1988. Witherspoon plays Annette Hargrove, the very proper and well-behaved daughter of the headmaster of a private school in New York City. Kathryn (Sarah Michele Gellar) and her stepbrother Sebastian (Ryan Phillippe) amuse themselves one summer by making bets with each other. Annette has announced that she intends to stay "pure" until she gets married. So Kathryn bets Sebastian that he won't be able to seduce her before school starts in the fall. *Variety* called Witherspoon's portrayal of Annette "a difficult role" in which she was outshone by her co-star Gellar. But filming *Cruel Intentions* proved to be a turning point in Witherspoon's personal life: not long after the film was released, she and Ryan Phillippe announced that they were expecting a baby and planned to get married.

> "I had to make a choice between Psych 101 and starring in a film opposite Paul Newman, Gene Hackman, Susan Sarandon, and James Garner. My parents didn't quite understand my decision, but to me it was a no-brainer."

Witherspoon's third movie during this very busy period in her life was the one that finally brought her the widespread critical acclaim she'd been hoping for. In *Election* she plays Tracy Flick, an ambitious over-achiever in a Nebraska high school who wants desperately to become class president so she can improve her chances of getting into a prestigious college. She's opposed by Mr. McAllister (Matthew Broderick), the teacher who acts as an advisor to the student government. He is so alienated by Tracy's single-minded pursuit of the position that he tries to undermine her plans by finding another student to run against her—and more. His actions cost him his job and his marriage, but Tracy emerges as the movie's most fasci-

Witherspoon as Tracy Flick in a scene from Election, *1999.*

nating character. One reviewer called her "Chirpy, clipped, coiled like a rat-tlesnake . . . The girl with complete homework, perfect hair, and sensible clothes who always thrusts her hand into the air like a Hitler salute when the teacher asks a question." Another described her as "a whole new kind of villain," so dead set on achieving her goal that she won't let anything stand in her way.

Although *Election* was only a modest box office success, it brought Wither-spoon her first Golden Globe nomination and a Best Actress award from the National Society of Film Critics. "Witherspoon nails Tracy in a nifty performance that all viewers will recognize as true," commented the re-viewer for *Variety*. "There's one of her ilk in every school and office." By this point, Witherspoon was starting to earn a reputation for her varied and nuanced performances in some unexpected films.

The critical success of *Election* was followed by a disappointment: *Best Laid Plans,* in which Witherspoon starred with Alessandro Nivola. Nick (Nivola) is a young man who'd like to escape his job at a recycling plant and run off with his girlfriend, Lissa (Witherspoon). But the only way he can get enough money to finance his dream is to help a friend who is planning a burglary. The friend gets caught, the stolen money disappears, and Nick and Lissa have to find a way to replace it. Critics didn't like the movie and said that even its stars weren't "big enough to power the material." But Witherspoon didn't let the poor reviews bother her as she gave birth to a daughter in September 1999, the same month the movie was released.

Legally Blonde

Witherspoon took some time off in late 1999 to undergo what she calls "a crash course in motherhood." But she was back at work the following year, appearing as Christian Bale's girl-friend in *American Psycho,* as a college girl who is seduced by her room-mate's father in *Slow Motion,* and as Adam Sandler's angelic mother in a slapstick film about Hell and Satan called *Little Nicky.* She also appeared as a guest star in two episodes of the television show "Friends," playing Jennifer Aniston's younger sister. But in 2001 her career took another giant leap forward when she appeared as Elle Woods in *Legally Blonde,* her first real box office hit.

> *Tracy Flick has been described as "Chirpy, clipped, coiled like a rattlesnake . . . The girl with complete homework, perfect hair, and sensible clothes who always thrusts her hand into the air like a Hitler salute when the teacher asks a question."*

Elle is a sorority girl and fashion major at a California college who is rich, popular, and determined to marry her boyfriend, Warner Huntington (Matt Davis). He is heading off to Harvard Law School, and she is eagerly antici-pating a marriage proposal before he goes. Elle is devastated when instead of proposing Warner dumps her, because he has political ambitions and doesn't think that Elle is smart enough or accomplished enough to be a senator's wife. Rather than admit defeat, she starts cramming for the Harvard Law entrance exam and manages to get accepted there herself. She arrives in Cambridge, among all the serious, snobby, and brilliant stu-dents at Harvard Law School, dressed like a California girl and carrying her pet Chihuahua. Determined to get Warner back by proving that she's more than a "dumb blonde," Elle ends up triumphing, winning the respect of her teachers and her fellow law students—and the affection of a large movie audience.

Witherspoon's performance in *Legally Blonde* was compared to Goldie Hawn's in *Private Benjamin* and Melanie Griffith's in *Working Girl,* two

*Scenes of
Witherspoon as
Elle Woods in*
Legally Blonde.

other movies about blondes who transform themselves into smart, successful women. A critic from *Variety* called her "a comedienne worthy of comparison to such golden era greats as Carole Lombard and Ginger Rogers" and proclaimed her "one of a very small number of screen actors one wants to see in anything she does." More importantly from a career standpoint, *Legally Blonde* was a huge box office hit, earning more than $100 million and catapulting Reese Witherspoon to nationwide fame. While some of her fans were surprised that she would play a "dumb blonde" after her interesting and complex roles in *Pleasantville* and *Election*, Witherspoon defended her choice. "Making *Legally Blonde* was my own private campaign against a lot of prejudices and stereotypes," she said.

> *"I had been playing characters that were larger than life, and I decided to do something that was a little more close to my own personality,"* Witherspoon said about filming **Sweet Home Alabama.** *"[Melanie's] a southern girl who moves away and makes an entirely new life for herself in this urban world, then has to go home again. Eventually, she grows to love what's beautiful about the place she came from and recognizes it as part of herself — maybe the best part of herself."*

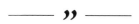

Recent Film Roles

In keeping with her determination to avoid being typecast, Witherspoon went from playing a California sorority girl to playing Cecily in *The Importance of Being Earnest*, the new film version of the 1895 Oscar Wilde play. In this classic comedy of errors story, two gents living in England in the 1890s have each bent the truth a bit, inventing a character named Earnest. But things start to go wrong as their lies are discovered. For Witherspoon, it was an enjoyable change of pace. "I haven't done a lot of period [films]," she explained, "and I saw it as a challenge." Even more challenging was learning to speak with an English accent, which took Witherspoon six weeks of study to master. She was the only American in an all-star British cast that included Colin Firth, Judi Dench, and Rupert Everett.

For her most recent film, *Sweet Home Alabama*, Witherspoon had to re-learn the southern accent she was born with. Released in September 2002, the romantic comedy *Sweet Home Alabama* tells the story of Melanie Car-michael, a southern girl who moves from Alabama to New York City and becomes a successful fashion designer. She's elated when her new boyfriend Andrew (Patrick Dempsey), who also happens to be the mayor's son and the city's most eligible bachelor, asks her to marry him. But Melanie is forced to return home and confront Jake (Josh Lucas), the man she married as a teenager and never officially divorced. Annoyed that Melanie has re-entered his life, Jake refuses to sign the divorce papers. In the struggle that ensues, Melanie and Jake discover that they are still attracted to one another, and she realizes that she loves both men. Melanie is forced to choose between the man who wants to marry her and the one to whom she has been married all along.

> *"I'm the classic Type A personality," Witherspoon explains, "because I have a strong tendency towards being compulsive and anxious."*

"I had been playing characters that were larger than life, and I decided to do something that was a little more close to my own personality," Witherspoon said in an interview. "[Melanie's] a southern girl who moves away and makes an entirely new life for herself in this urban world, then has to go home again. Eventually, she grows to love what's beautiful about the place she came from and recognizes it as part of herself — maybe the best part of herself."

The movie proved to be a bit of a disappointment, earning mixed reviews — some good, but some rather unenthusiastic. *The New Yorker*, for example, panned the movie but praised Witherspoon by saying, "Among the many talents of Reese Witherspoon is the ability to hang around in movies that are unworthy of her, and thus to shine all the brighter." Despite the film's lukewarm reviews, however, it earned $37.5 million the first weekend it opened.

Future Plans and Projects

"I am very ambitious and very focused—that's the kind of character I gravitate toward," Witherspoon explains. "I also feel a responsibility as an actress to represent women in a way that I want to be represented." With this goal in mind, she has recently started her own production company, called Type A Films after her mother's nickname for her. "I'm the classic Type A personality," she explains, "because I have a strong tendency towards being compulsive and anxious." Type A's first film project, which is sched-

Witherspoon with two of her co-stars from Sweet Home Alabama: *Patrick Dempsey, left (Andrew, her fiancé), and Josh Lucas, right (Jake, her husband).*

uled to be released in 2003, is a sequel to *Legally Blonde* called *Red, White, and Blonde,* which Witherspoon has directed and stars in. Soon after that, she will appear in the lead role of an independent period film based on the 1848 novel *Vanity Fair* by William Makepeace Thackeray.

Type A Films is currently working on a film adaptation of Melissa Bank's best-selling 1999 novel, *The Girl's Guide to Hunting and Fishing,* which Witherspoon will produce and star in. She is also working on a movie about women's professional tennis—"I'm in awe of female athletes," she says. Other projects include playing Honey West in a film based on the 1960s television series about a woman detective. As both an actress and a producer, Witherspoon remains committed to making small, independent films. If things don't work out for her in Hollywood, she says, "I'll go to medical school."

MARRIAGE AND FAMILY

Witherspoon knew Ryan Phillippe before she worked with him on *Cruel Intentions.* She met him at her own 21st birthday party, to which a friend had invited him. Witherspoon readily admits that her pregnancy was not planned and that, at 23, she was unprepared for motherhood. But Phillippe's mother had run a day care center, and he had a lot of experience handling infants and changing diapers.

159

Witherspoon and Phillippe were married on June 5, 1999, and their daughter, Ava Elizabeth, was born on September 9. "She really encouraged me to grow up, become more mature," Witherspoon says. She and her husband and daughter now live in Hollywood Hills with their English bulldog. Despite the demands of their busy acting careers, they try to spend no more than a week or two away from Ava or from each other. "We like to cook dinner every night and take our daughter to school every day. We have a pretty normal life outside of the movie stuff," Witherspoon says. Now that Ava is almost four years old, Witherspoon credits her with taking "all the self-obsession out of my life." Her family life is a source of strength for her. "I feel very blessed," she says. "Every day of my life I think God that I found someone that I'm so in love with and we have such a wonderful life. It's really nice to connect with someone on pretty much everything."

MAJOR INFLUENCES

Witherspoon's role models have always been not only actresses, but strong, independent women who have worked hard to make a name for themselves. She calls Jodie Foster, Susan Sarandon, Holly Hunter, and Frances McDormand "actresses who consistently do great work despite ageism and all sorts of other factors working against them." As a comedienne, Witherspoon says that she has been influenced by Lucille Ball, Carol Burnett, and Goldie Hawn.

CREDITS

Films

The Man in the Moon, 1991
Jack the Bear, 1993
A Far Off Place, 1993
S.F.W., 1994
Fear, 1996

Overnight Delivery, 1996
Freeway, 1996
Twilight, 1998
Pleasantville, 1998
Cruel Intentions, 1999
Election, 1999
Best Laid Plans, 1999
American Psycho, 2000
Little Nicky, 2000
Slow Motion, 2000
Legally Blonde, 2001
The Importance of Being Earnest, 2002
Sweet Home Alabama, 2002

Television

Wildflower, 1991
Desperate Choices: To Save My Child, 1992
"Return to Lonesome Dove," 1993
"Friends," 1999

SELECTED HONORS AND AWARDS

Best Actress (National Society of Film Critics): 1999, for *Election*
Best Actress (Kansas City Film Critics Circle): 2000, for *Election*
Blockbuster Entertainment Award: 2000, Favorite Supporting Actress-
   Drama/Romance, for *Cruel Intentions*
MTV Movie Award: 2002, Best Comedic Performance, for *Legally Blonde*
Teen Choice Award for Extraordinary Achievement: 2002

FURTHER READING

Books

Contemporary Theatre, Film, and Television, Vol. 31, 2000

Periodicals

Biography, June 2002, p.38
Cosmopolitan, July 2001, p.170
Entertainment Weekly, Oct. 11, 1996, p.99; Oct. 14, 2002, p.77
In Style, Oct.. 1, 2002, p.458
Interview, Nov. 1994, p.116

Newsweek, Apr. 26, 1999, p.66
People, Oct. 14, 2002, p.77
Premiere, Aug. 2001, p.44
Seventeen, Oct. 2002, p.166
Teen, May 1995, p.90; Sep. 2001, p.50
Time, Aug. 6, 2001, p.58
Times (London), Aug. 25, 2002, Features section, p.6; Dec. 14, 2002, Features Section, p.42
Vanity Fair, June. 2000, p.172
W, Sep. 2002, p.416

Online Database

Biography Resource Center Online, 2003, article from *Contemporary Theatre, Film, and Television,* 2000

ADDRESS

Reese Witherspoon
Universal Studios
Type A Films
100 Universal City Plaza
Universal City, CA 91608

Photo and Illustration Credits

Yolanda Adams/Photos: Marc Baptiste; AP/Wide World Photos; copyright © Reuters NewMedia Inc./CORBIS. CD covers: *Believe* copyright © 2001 Elektra Entertainment Group Inc.; *More Than a Melody* (p) & © 1997 Zomba Recording Corporation; *Mountain High . . . Valley Low* copyright © 1999 Elektra Entertainment Group Inc; *Through the Storm* (p) & © 1997 Zomba Recording Corporation.

Laura Bush/Photos: George Bush Presidential Library; Greg Mathieson/ MAI/TIMEPIX; White House/TIMEPIX; AP/Wide World Photos. Cover: AP/Wide World Photos.

Eminem/Photos: AP/Wide World Photos; Eli Reed; AP/Wide World Photos. CD covers: *The Eminem Show* (p) © 2002 Aftermath Records; *The Marshall Mathers LP* (p) © 2000 Aftermath Entertainment/Interscope Records; *The Slim Shady LP* copyright © 1999 Aftermath Entertainment/Interscope Records.

Vicente Fox/Photos: copyright © Reuters NewMedia Inc./CORBIS; AP/ Wide World Photos. Cover: copyright © AFP/CORBIS.

Millard Fuller/Photos: Kim MacDonald/Habitat for Humanity International; Robert Baker/Habitat for Humanity International; AP/Wide World Photos; Kim MacDonald/Habitat for Humanity International.

Jeanette Lee/Photos: Layne Kennedy/TIMEPIX; AP/Wide World Photos; George De Sota/Getty Images;.

Clint Mathis/Photos: Steve Smith/2002; Aubrey Washington/Getty Images; Stephen Dunn/Getty Images; Steve Smith/2002; copyright © Duomo/COR-BIS; AP/Wide World Photos; Michael Stahlschmidt/SSI/TIMEPIX; Jeff Gross/ Getty Images.

Donovan McNabb/Photos: Ezra Shaw/Getty Images; Rick Stewart/Getty Images; Ezra Shaw/Getty Images; AP/Wide World Photos. Cover: AP/Wide World Photos.

Emma Watson/Photos: Lawrence Lucier/Getty Images; Peter Mountain; copyright © Reuters NewMedia Inc./CORBIS; © 2002 Warner Brothers.

Reese Witherspoon/Photos: copyright © Rufus F. Folkks/CORBIS; Ralph Nelson/New Line Cinema; copyright © CORBIS Sygma; copyright © 2001 Metro-Golden-Mayer Pictures, Inc.; Timothy White. DVD cover: copyright © 1991 Metro-Golden-Mayer Studios Inc.

How to Use the Cumulative Index

Our indexes have a new look. In an effort to make our indexes easier to use, we've combined the Name and General Index into a new, Cumulative Index. This single ready-reference resource covers all the volumes in *Biography Today*, both the general series and the special subject series. The new Cumulative Index contains complete listings of all individuals who have appeared in *Biography Today* since the series began. Their names appear in bold-faced type, followed by the issue in which they appear. The Cumulative Index also includes references for the occupations, nationalities, and ethnic and minority origins of individuals profiled in *Biography Today*.

We have also made some changes to our specialty indexes, the Places of Birth Index and the Birthday Index. To consolidate and to save space, the Places of Birth Index and the Birthday Index will no longer appear in the January and April issues of the softbound subscription series. But these indexes can still be found in the September issue of the softbound subscription series, in the hardbound Annual Cumulation at the end of each year, and in each volume of the special subject series.

General Series

The General Series of *Biography Today* is denoted in the index with the month and year of the issue in which the individual appeared. Each individual also appears in the Annual Cumulation for that year.

Special Subject Series

The Special Subject Series of *Biography Today* are each denoted in the index with an abbreviated form of the series name, plus the number of the volume in which the individual appears. They are listed as follows.

Adams, Ansel . . . . Artist V.1   (Artists Series)
Cabot, Meg. . . . . Author V.12   (Author Series)
Chan, Jackie. . . . . PerfArt V.1   (Performing Artists Series)
Fauci, Anthony. . . . . Science V.7   (Scientists & Inventors Series)
Moseley, Jonny . . . . Sport V.8   (Sports Series)
Peterson, Roger Tory . . . . WorLdr V.1   (World Leaders Series: Environmental Leaders)
Sadat, Anwar . . . . WorLdr V.2   (World Leaders Series: Modern African Leaders)
Wolf, Hazel. . . . . WorLdr V.3   (World Leaders Series: Environmental Leaders 2)

Updates

Updated information on selected individuals appears in the Appendix at the end of the *Biography Today* Annual Cumulation. In the index, the original entry is listed first, followed by any updates.

Arafat, Yasir . . . . Sep 94; Update 94; Update 95; Update 96; Update 97; Update 98; Update 00; Update 01; Update 02
Gates, Bill . . . . Apr 93; Update 98; Update 00; Science V.5; Update 01
Griffith Joyner, Florence. . . . . Sport V.1; Update 98
Sanders, Barry . . . . Sep 95; Update 99
Spock, Dr. Benjamin . . . . Sep 95; Update 98
Yeltsin, Boris . . . . Apr 92; Update 93; Update 95; Update 96; Update 98; Update 00

Cumulative Index

This cumulative index includes names, occupations, nationalities, and ethnic and minority origins that pertain to all individuals profiled in *Biography Today* since the debut of the series in 1992.

CUMULATIVE INDEX

Sosa, Sammy . . . . Jan 99; Update 99
Soto, Gary . . . . Author V.5
South Africans
  de Klerk, F.W. . . . . Apr 94; Update 94
  Mandela, Nelson. . . . . . . Jan 92; Update 94;
    Update 01
  Mandela, Winnie . . . . WorLdr V.2
South Korean
  Pak, Se Ri . . . . Sport V.4
Spaniards
  Domingo, Placido. . . . . Sep 95
  Garcia, Sergio . . . . Sport V.7
  Iglesias, Enrique. . . . . Jan 03
  Sanchez Vicario, Arantxa . . . . . . Sport V.1
Speare, Elizabeth George. . . . . Sep 95
Spears, Britney . . . . Jan 01
spelling bee competition
  Andrews, Ned. . . . . Sep 94
  Guey, Wendy . . . . Sep 96
  Hooper, Geoff . . . . Jan 94
  Maxwell, Jody-Anne . . . . Sep 98
  Sealfon, Rebecca. . . . . Sep 97
  Thampy, George. . . . . Sep 00
Spelman, Lucy . . . . Science V.6
Spencer, Diana
  see Diana, Princess of Wales. . . . . Jul 92;
    Update 96; Update 97; Jan 98
Spielberg, Steven. . . . . . . Jan 94; Update 94;
  Update 95
Spinelli, Jerry . . . . Apr 93
Spock, Dr. Benjamin. . . . Sep 95; Update 98
sports
  Aaron, Hank. . . . . Sport V.1
  Abdul-Jabbar, Kareem. . . . . Sport V.1
  Agassi, Andre . . . . Jul 92
  Aikman, Troy. . . . . Apr 95; Update 01
  Ali, Muhammad. . . . . Sport V.2
  Allen, Marcus . . . . Sep 97
  Ammann, Simon . . . . Sport V.8
  Andretti, Mario . . . . Sep 94
  Armstrong, Lance. . . . . . Sep 00; Update 00;
    Update 01; Update 02
  Ashe, Arthur . . . . Sep 93
  Bahrke, Shannon . . . . Sport V.8
  Bailey, Donovan. . . . . Sport V.2
  Baiul, Oksana . . . . Apr 95
  Barkley, Charles . . . . Apr 92; Update 02
  Bird, Larry. . . . . Jan 92; Update 98
  Blair, Bonnie . . . . Apr 94
  Bonds, Barry. . . . . Jan 03
  Boulmerka, Hassiba. . . . . Sport V.1

Brady, Tom . . . . Sport V.7
Bryant, Kobe . . . . Apr 99
Butcher, Susan . . . . Sport V.1
Capriati, Jennifer . . . . Sport V.6
Carter, Vince. . . . . . . Sport V.5; Update 01
Chamberlain, Wilt . . . . Sport V.4
Chastain, Brandi. . . . . Sport V.4; Update 00
Clark, Kelly . . . . Sport V.8
Dakides, Tara . . . . Sport V.7
Daniel, Beth . . . . Sport V.1
Davenport, Lindsay . . . . Sport V.5
Dayne, Ron . . . . Apr 00
Devers, Gail . . . . Sport V.2
Dragila, Stacy . . . . Sport V.6
Driscoll, Jean . . . . Sep 97
Dumars, Joe. . . . . Sport V.3; Update 99
Dunlap, Alison . . . . Sport V.7
Earnhardt, Dale. . . . . Apr 01
Elway, John . . . . Sport V.2; Update 99
Evans, Janet . . . . Jan 95
Evert, Chris . . . . Sport V.1
Ewing, Patrick . . . . Jan 95; Update 02
Favre, Brett . . . . Sport V.2
Fedorov, Sergei . . . . Apr 94; Update 94
Fernandez, Lisa . . . . Sport V.5
Flowers, Vonetta. . . . . Sport V.8
Freeman, Cathy . . . . Jan 01
Fu Mingxia . . . . Sport V.5
Garcia, Sergio . . . . Sport V.7
Garnett, Kevin . . . . Sport V.6
George, Eddie. . . . . Sport V.6
Gordon, Jeff. . . . . Apr 99
Graf, Steffi. . . . . Jan 92; Update 01
Granato, Cammi. . . . . Sport V.8
Gretzky, Wayne . . . . Jan 92; Update 93;
  Update 99
Griese, Brian. . . . . Jan 02
Griffey, Ken, Jr. . . . . Sport V.1
Griffith Joyner, Florence. . . . . Sport V.1;
  Update 98
Hamm, Mia. . . . . Sport V.2; Update 00
Harbaugh, Jim . . . . Sport V.3
Hardaway, Anfernee "Penny" . . . Sport V.2
Harding, Tonya. . . . . Sep 94
Hasek, Dominik . . . . Sport V.3
Hawk, Tony. . . . . Apr 01
Hernandez, Livan. . . . . Apr 98
Hill, Grant. . . . . Sport V.1
Hingis, Martina . . . . Sport V.2
Hogan, Hulk . . . . Apr 92

Biography Today
General Series

For ages 9 and above

Biography Today **General Series** includes a unique combination of current biographical profiles that teachers and librarians — and the readers themselves — tell us are most appealing. The **General Series** is available as a 3-issue subscription; hardcover annual cumulation; or subscription plus cumulation.

Within the **General Series**, your readers will find a variety of sketches about:

- Authors
- Musicians
- Political leaders
- Sports figures
- Movie actresses & actors
- Cartoonists
- Scientists
- Astronauts
- TV personalities
- and the movers & shakers in many other fields!

"Biography Today **will be useful in elementary and middle school libraries and in public library children's collections where there is a need for biographies of current personalities. High schools serving reluctant readers may also want to consider a subscription."**
— *Booklist,* American Library Association

"Highly recommended for the young adult audience. Readers will delight in the accessible, energetic, tell-all style; teachers, librarians, and parents will welcome the clever format, intelligent and informative text. It should prove especially useful in motivating 'reluctant' readers or literate nonreaders."
— *MultiCultural Review*

"Written in a friendly, almost chatty tone, the profiles offer quick, objective information. While coverage of current figures makes *Biography Today* **a useful reference tool, an appealing format and wide scope make it a fun resource to browse."**   — *School Library Journal*

"The best source for current information at a level kids can understand."
— Kelly Bryant, School Librarian, Carlton, OR

"Easy for kids to read. We love it! Don't want to be without it."
— Lynn McWhirter, School Librarian, Rockford, IL

ONE-YEAR SUBSCRIPTION
- 3 softcover issues, 6" x 9"
- Published in January, April, and September
- 1-year subscription, $57
- 150 pages per issue
- 8-10 profiles per issue
- Contact sources for additional information
- Cumulative General, Places of Birth, and Birthday Indexes

HARDBOUND ANNUAL CUMULATION
- Sturdy 6" x 9" hardbound volume
- Published in December
- $58 per volume
- 450 pages per volume
- 25-30 profiles — includes all profiles found in softcover issues for that calendar year
- Cumulative General, Places of Birth, and Birthday Indexes
- Special appendix features current updates of previous profiles

SUBSCRIPTION AND CUMULATION COMBINATION
- $99 for 3 softcover issues plus the hardbound volume

1992

Paula Abdul
Andre Agassi
Kirstie Alley
Terry Anderson
Roseanne Arnold
Isaac Asimov
James Baker
Charles Barkley
Larry Bird
Judy Blume
Berke Breathed
Garth Brooks
Barbara Bush
George Bush
Fidel Castro
Bill Clinton
Bill Cosby
Diana, Princess of Wales
Shannen Doherty
Elizabeth Dole
David Duke
Gloria Estefan
Mikhail Gorbachev
Steffi Graf
Wayne Gretzky
Matt Groening
Alex Haley
Hammer
Martin Handford
Stephen Hawking
Hulk Hogan
Saddam Hussein
Lee Iacocca
Bo Jackson
Mae Jemison
Peter Jennings
Steven Jobs
Pope John Paul II
Magic Johnson
Michael Jordon
Jackie Joyner-Kersee
Spike Lee
Mario Lemieux
Madeleine L'Engle
Jay Leno
Yo-Yo Ma
Nelson Mandela
Wynton Marsalis
Thurgood Marshall
Ann Martin
Barbara McClintock
Emily Arnold McCully
Antonia Novello

Sandra Day O'Connor
Rosa Parks
Jane Pauley
H. Ross Perot
Luke Perry
Scottie Pippen
Colin Powell
Jason Priestley
Queen Latifah
Yitzhak Rabin
Sally Ride
Pete Rose
Nolan Ryan
H. Norman
 Schwarzkopf
Jerry Seinfeld
Dr. Seuss
Gloria Steinem
Clarence Thomas
Chris Van Allsburg
Cynthia Voigt
Bill Watterson
Robin Williams
Oprah Winfrey
Kristi Yamaguchi
Boris Yeltsin

1993

Maya Angelou
Arthur Ashe
Avi
Kathleen Battle
Candice Bergen
Boutros Boutros-Ghali
Chris Burke
Dana Carvey
Cesar Chavez
Henry Cisneros
Hillary Rodham Clinton
Jacques Cousteau
Cindy Crawford
Macaulay Culkin
Lois Duncan
Marian Wright Edelman
Cecil Fielder
Bill Gates
Sara Gilbert
Dizzy Gillespie
Al Gore
Cathy Guisewite
Jasmine Guy
Anita Hill
Ice-T
Darci Kistler

k.d. lang
Dan Marino
Rigoberta Menchu
Walter Dean Myers
Martina Navratilova
Phyllis Reynolds Naylor
Rudolf Nureyev
Shaquille O'Neal
Janet Reno
Jerry Rice
Mary Robinson
Winona Ryder
Jerry Spinelli
Denzel Washington
Keenen Ivory Wayans
Dave Winfield

1994

Tim Allen
Marian Anderson
Mario Andretti
Ned Andrews
Yasir Arafat
Bruce Babbitt
Mayim Bialik
Bonnie Blair
Ed Bradley
John Candy
Mary Chapin Carpenter
Benjamin Chavis
Connie Chung
Beverly Cleary
Kurt Cobain
F.W. de Klerk
Rita Dove
Linda Ellerbee
Sergei Fedorov
Zlata Filipovic
Daisy Fuentes
Ruth Bader Ginsburg
Whoopi Goldberg
Tonya Harding
Melissa Joan Hart
Geoff Hooper
Whitney Houston
Dan Jansen
Nancy Kerrigan
Alexi Lalas
Charlotte Lopez
Wilma Mankiller
Shannon Miller
Toni Morrison
Richard Nixon
Greg Norman
Severo Ochoa

River Phoenix
Elizabeth Pine
Jonas Salk
Richard Scarry
Emmitt Smith
Will Smith
Steven Spielberg
Patrick Stewart
R.L. Stine
Lewis Thomas
Barbara Walters
Charlie Ward
Steve Young
Kim Zmeskal

1995

Troy Aikman
Jean-Bertrand Aristide
Oksana Baiul
Halle Berry
Benazir Bhutto
Jonathan Brandis
Warren E. Burger
Ken Burns
Candace Cameron
Jimmy Carter
Agnes de Mille
Placido Domingo
Janet Evans
Patrick Ewing
Newt Gingrich
John Goodman
Amy Grant
Jesse Jackson
James Earl Jones
Julie Krone
David Letterman
Rush Limbaugh
Heather Locklear
Reba McEntire
Joe Montana
Cosmas Ndeti
Hakeem Olajuwon
Ashley Olsen
Mary-Kate Olsen
Jennifer Parkinson
Linus Pauling
Itzhak Perlman
Cokie Roberts
Wilma Rudolph
Salt 'N' Pepa
Barry Sanders
William Shatner
Elizabeth George
 Speare

Dr. Benjamin Spock
Jonathan Taylor
  Thomas
Vicki Van Meter
Heather Whitestone
Pedro Zamora

1996

Aung San Suu Kyi
Boyz II Men
Brandy
Ron Brown
Mariah Carey
Jim Carrey
Larry Champagne III
Christo
Chelsea Clinton
Coolio
Bob Dole
David Duchovny
Debbi Fields
Chris Galeczka
Jerry Garcia
Jennie Garth
Wendy Guey
Tom Hanks
Alison Hargreaves
Sir Edmund Hillary
Judith Jamison
Barbara Jordan
Annie Leibovitz
Carl Lewis
Jim Lovell
Mickey Mantle
Lynn Margulis
Iqbal Masih
Mark Messier
Larisa Oleynik
Christopher Pike
David Robinson
Dennis Rodman
Selena
Monica Seles
Don Shula
Kerri Strug
Tiffani-Amber Thiessen
Dave Thomas
Jaleel White

1997

Madeleine Albright
Marcus Allen
Gillian Anderson
Rachel Blanchard
Zachery Ty Bryan
Adam Ezra Cohen
Claire Danes
Celine Dion
Jean Driscoll
Louis Farrakhan
Ella Fitzgerald
Harrison Ford
Bryant Gumbel
John Johnson
Michael Johnson
Maya Lin
George Lucas
John Madden
Bill Monroe
Alanis Morissette
Sam Morrison
Rosie O'Donnell
Muammar el-Qaddafi
Christopher Reeve
Pete Sampras
Pat Schroeder
Rebecca Sealfon
Tupac Shakur
Tabitha Soren
Herbert Tarvin
Merlin Tuttle
Mara Wilson

1998

Bella Abzug
Kofi Annan
Neve Campbell
Sean Combs (Puff
  Daddy)
Dalai Lama (Tenzin
  Gyatso)
Diana, Princess of Wales
Leonardo DiCaprio
Walter E. Diemer
Ruth Handler
Hanson
Livan Hernandez
Jewel
Jimmy Johnson
Tara Lipinski
Jody-Anne Maxwell
Dominique Moceanu
Alexandra Nechita

Brad Pitt
LeAnn Rimes
Emily Rosa
David Satcher
Betty Shabazz
Kordell Stewart
Shinichi Suzuki
Mother Teresa
Mike Vernon
Reggie White
Kate Winslet

1999

Ben Affleck
Jennifer Aniston
Maurice Ashley
Kobe Bryant
Bessie Delany
Sadie Delany
Sharon Draper
Sarah Michelle Gellar
John Glenn
Savion Glover
Jeff Gordon
David Hampton
Lauryn Hill
King Hussein
Lynn Johnston
Shari Lewis
Oseola McCarty
Mark McGwire
Slobodan Milosevic
Natalie Portman
J. K. Rowling
Frank Sinatra
Gene Siskel
Sammy Sosa
John Stanford
Natalia Toro
Shania Twain
Mitsuko Uchida
Jesse Ventura
Venus Williams

2000

Christina Aguilera
K.A. Applegate
Lance Armstrong
Backstreet Boys
Daisy Bates
Harry Blackmun
George W. Bush
Carson Daly
Ron Dayne
Henry Louis Gates, Jr.
Doris Haddock
  (Granny D)
Jennifer Love Hewitt
Chamique Holdsclaw
Katie Holmes
Charlayne Hunter-Gault
Johanna Johnson
Craig Kielburger
John Lasseter
Peyton Manning
Ricky Martin
John McCain
Walter Payton
Freddie Prinze, Jr.
Viviana Risca
Briana Scurry
George Thampy
CeCe Winans

2001

Jessica Alba
Christiane Amanpour
Drew Barrymore
Jeff Bezos
Destiny's Child
Dale Earnhardt
Carly Fiorina
Aretha Franklin
Cathy Freeman
Tony Hawk
Faith Hill
Kim Dae-jung
Madeleine L'Engle
Mariangela Lisanti
Frankie Muniz
*N Sync
Ellen Ochoa
Jeff Probst
Julia Roberts
Carl T. Rowan
Britney Spears
Chris Tucker
Lloyd D. Ward
Alan Webb
Chris Weinke

2002

Aaliyah
Osama bin Laden
Mary J. Blige
Aubyn Burnside
Aaron Carter
Julz Chavez
Dick Cheney
Hilary Duff
Billy Gilman
Rudolph Giuliani
Brian Griese
Jennifer Lopez
Dave Mirra
Dineh Mohajer
Leanne Nakamura
Daniel Radcliffe
Condoleezza Rice
Marla Runyan
Ruth Simmons
Mattie Stepanek
J.R.R. Tolkien
Barry Watson
Tyrone Willingham
Elijah Wood

2003

Yolanda Adams
Mildred Benson
Alexis Bledel
Barry Bonds
Laura Bush
Kelly Clarkson
Vin Diesel
Eminem
Michele Forman
Vicente Fox
Millard Fuller
Sarah Hughes
Enrique Iglesias
Jeanette Lee
John Lewis
Clint Mathis
Donovan McNabb
Andy Roddick
Emma Watson
Reese Witherspoon

Biography Today

For ages 9 and above

Subject Series

Expands and complements the General Series and targets specific subject areas . . .

Our readers asked for it! They wanted more biographies, and the *Biography Today* **Subject Series** is our response to that demand. Now your readers can choose their special areas of interest and go on to read about their favorites in those fields. Priced at just $39 per volume, the following specific volumes are included in the *Biography Today* **Subject Series**:

- **Artists**
- **Authors**
- **Performing Artists**
- **Scientists & Inventors**
- **Sports**
- **World Leaders**
  Environmental Leaders
  Modern African Leaders

FEATURES AND FORMAT

- Sturdy 6" x 9" hardbound volumes
- Individual volumes, $39 each
- 200 pages per volume
- 10-12 profiles per volume — targets individuals within a specific subject area
- Contact sources for additional information
- Cumulative General, Places of Birth, and Birthday Indexes

NOTE: There is *no duplication of entries* between the **General Series** of *Biography Today* and the **Subject Series**.

AUTHOR SERIES

"A useful tool for children's assignment needs." — *School Library Journal*

"The prose is workmanlike: report writers will find enough detail to begin sound investigations, and browsers are likely to find someone of interest." — *School Library Journal*

SCIENTISTS & INVENTORS SERIES

"The articles are readable, attractively laid out, and touch on important points that will suit assignment needs. Browsers will note the clear writing and interesting details."
— *School Library Journal*

"The book is excellent for demonstrating that scientists are real people with widely diverse backgrounds and personal interests. The biographies are fascinating to read."
— *The Science Teacher*

SPORTS SERIES

"This series should become a standard resource in libraries that serve intermediate students." — *School Library Journal*

ENVIRONMENTAL LEADERS #1

"A tremendous book that fills a gap in the biographical category of books. This is a great reference book." — *Science Scope*

Artists

VOLUME 1

Ansel Adams
Romare Bearden
Margaret Bourke-White
Alexander Calder
Marc Chagall
Helen Frankenthaler
Jasper Johns
Jacob Lawrence
Henry Moore
Grandma Moses
Louise Nevelson
Georgia O'Keeffe
Gordon Parks
I.M. Pei
Diego Rivera
Norman Rockwell
Andy Warhol
Frank Lloyd Wright

Authors

VOLUME 1

Eric Carle
Alice Childress
Robert Cormier
Roald Dahl
Jim Davis
John Grisham
Virginia Hamilton
James Herriot
S.E. Hinton
M.E. Kerr
Stephen King
Gary Larson
Joan Lowery Nixon
Gary Paulsen
Cynthia Rylant
Mildred D. Taylor
Kurt Vonnegut, Jr.
E.B. White
Paul Zindel

VOLUME 2

James Baldwin
Stan and Jan Berenstain
David Macaulay
Patricia MacLachlan
Scott O'Dell
Jerry Pinkney
Jack Prelutsky

Lynn Reid Banks
Faith Ringgold
J.D. Salinger
Charles Schulz
Maurice Sendak
P.L. Travers
Garth Williams

VOLUME 3

Candy Dawson Boyd
Ray Bradbury
Gwendolyn Brooks
Ralph W. Ellison
Louise Fitzhugh
Jean Craighead George
E.L. Konigsburg
C.S. Lewis
Fredrick L. McKissack
Patricia C. McKissack
Katherine Paterson
Anne Rice
Shel Silverstein
Laura Ingalls Wilder

VOLUME 4

Betsy Byars
Chris Carter
Caroline B. Cooney
Christopher Paul Curtis
Anne Frank
Robert Heinlein
Marguerite Henry
Lois Lowry
Melissa Mathison
Bill Peet
August Wilson

VOLUME 5

Sharon Creech
Michael Crichton
Karen Cushman
Tomie dePaola
Lorraine Hansberry
Karen Hesse
Brian Jacques
Gary Soto
Richard Wright
Laurence Yep

VOLUME 6

Lloyd Alexander
Paula Danziger
Nancy Farmer
Zora Neale Hurston

Shirley Jackson
Angela Johnson
Jon Krakauer
Leo Lionni
Francine Pascal
Louis Sachar
Kevin Williamson

VOLUME 7

William H. Armstrong
Patricia Reilly Giff
Langston Hughes
Stan Lee
Julius Lester
Robert Pinsky
Todd Strasser
Jacqueline Woodson
Patricia C. Wrede
Jane Yolen

VOLUME 8

Amelia Atwater-Rhodes
Barbara Cooney
Paul Laurence Dunbar
Ursula K. Le Guin
Farley Mowat
Naomi Shihab Nye
Daniel Pinkwater
Beatrix Potter
Ann Rinaldi

VOLUME 9

Robb Armstrong
Cherie Bennett
Bruce Coville
Rosa Guy
Harper Lee
Irene Gut Opdyke
Philip Pullman
Jon Scieszka
Amy Tan
Joss Whedon

VOLUME 10

David Almond
Joan Bauer
Kate DiCamillo
Jack Gantos
Aaron McGruder
Richard Peck
Andrea Davis Pinkney
Louise Rennison
David Small
Katie Tarbox

VOLUME 11

Laurie Halse Anderson
Bryan Collier
Margaret Peterson
  Haddix
Milton Meltzer
William Sleator
Sonya Sones
Genndy Tartakovsky
Wendelin Van Draanen
Ruth White

VOLUME 12

An Na
Claude Brown
Meg Cabot
Virginia Hamilton
Chuck Jones
Robert Lipsyte
Lillian Morrison
Linda Sue Park
Pam Muñoz Ryan
Lemony Snicket
  (Daniel Handler)

VOLUME 13

Andrew Clements
Eoin Colfer
Sharon Flake
Edward Gorey
Francisco Jiménez
Astrid Lindgren
Chris Lynch
Marilyn Nelson
Tamora Pierce
Virginia Euwer Wolff

Performing Artists

VOLUME 1

Jackie Chan
Dixie Chicks
Kirsten Dunst
Suzanne Farrell
Bernie Mac
Shakira
Isaac Stern
Julie Taymor
Usher
Christina Vidal

Scientists & Inventors

VOLUME 1
John Bardeen
Sylvia Earle
Dian Fossey
Jane Goodall
Bernadine Healy
Jack Horner
Mathilde Krim
Edwin Land
Louise & Mary Leakey
Rita Levi-Montalcini
J. Robert Oppenheimer
Albert Sabin
Carl Sagan
James D. Watson

VOLUME 2
Jane Brody
Seymour Cray
Paul Erdös
Walter Gilbert
Stephen Jay Gould
Shirley Ann Jackson
Raymond Kurzweil
Shannon Lucid
Margaret Mead
Garrett Morgan
Bill Nye
Eloy Rodriguez
An Wang

VOLUME 3
Luis W. Alvarez
Hans A. Bethe
Gro Harlem Brundtland
Mary S. Calderone
Ioana Dumitriu
Temple Grandin
John Langston Gwaltney
Bernard Harris
Jerome Lemelson
Susan Love
Ruth Patrick
Oliver Sacks
Richie Stachowski

VOLUME 4
David Attenborough
Robert Ballard
Ben Carson
Eileen Collins
Biruté Galdikas
Lonnie Johnson
Meg Lowman
Forrest Mars Sr.
Akio Morita
Janese Swanson

VOLUME 5
Steve Case
Douglas Engelbart
Shawn Fanning
Sarah Flannery
Bill Gates
Laura Groppe
Grace Murray Hopper
Steven Jobs
Rand and Robyn Miller
Shigeru Miyamoto
Steve Wozniak

VOLUME 6
Hazel Barton
Alexa Canady
Arthur Caplan
Francis Collins
Gertrude Elion
Henry Heimlich
David Ho
Kenneth Kamler
Lucy Spelman
Lydia Villa-Komaroff

VOLUME 7
Tim Berners-Lee
France Córdova
Anthony S. Fauci
Sue Hendrickson
Steve Irwin
John Forbes Nash, Jr.
Jerri Nielsen
Ryan Patterson
Nina Vasan
Gloria WilderBrathwaite

Sports

VOLUME 1
Hank Aaron
Kareem Abdul-Jabbar
Hassiba Boulmerka
Susan Butcher
Beth Daniel
Chris Evert
Ken Griffey, Jr.
Florence Griffith Joyner
Grant Hill
Greg LeMond
Pelé
Uta Pippig
Cal Ripken, Jr.
Arantxa Sanchez Vicario
Deion Sanders
Tiger Woods

VOLUME 2
Muhammad Ali
Donovan Bailey
Gail Devers
John Elway
Brett Favre
Mia Hamm
Anfernee "Penny" Hardaway
Martina Hingis
Gordie Howe
Jack Nicklaus
Richard Petty
Dot Richardson
Sheryl Swoopes
Steve Yzerman

VOLUME 3
Joe Dumars
Jim Harbaugh
Dominik Hasek
Michelle Kwan
Rebecca Lobo
Greg Maddux
Fatuma Roba
Jackie Robinson
John Stockton
Picabo Street
Pat Summitt
Amy Van Dyken

VOLUME 4
Wilt Chamberlain
Brandi Chastain
Derek Jeter
Karch Kiraly
Alex Lowe
Randy Moss
Se Ri Pak
Dawn Riley
Karen Smyers
Kurt Warner
Serena Williams

VOLUME 5
Vince Carter
Lindsay Davenport
Lisa Fernandez
Fu Mingxia
Jaromir Jagr
Marion Jones
Pedro Martinez
Warren Sapp
Jenny Thompson
Karrie Webb

VOLUME 6
Jennifer Capriati
Stacy Dragila
Kevin Garnett
Eddie George
Alex Rodriguez
Joe Sakic
Annika Sorenstam
Jackie Stiles
Tiger Woods
Aliy Zirkle

VOLUME 7
Tom Brady
Tara Dakides
Alison Dunlap
Sergio Garcia
Allen Iverson
Shirley Muldowney
Ty Murray
Patrick Roy
Tasha Schwiker

VOLUME 8
Simon Ammann
Shannon Bahrke
Kelly Clark
Vonetta Flowers
Cammi Granato
Chris Klug
Jonny Moseley
Apolo Ohno
Sylke Otto
Ryne Sanborn
Jim Shea, Jr.

World Leaders

VOLUME 1: Environmental Leaders 1

Edward Abbey
Renee Askins
David Brower
Rachel Carson
Marjory Stoneman
    Douglas
Dave Foreman
Lois Gibbs
Wangari Maathai
Chico Mendes
Russell A. Mittermeier
Margaret and Olaus J.
    Murie
Patsy Ruth Oliver
Roger Tory Peterson
Ken Saro-Wiwa
Paul Watson
Adam Werbach

VOLUME 2: Modern African Leaders

Mohammed Farah
    Aidid
Idi Amin
Hastings Kamuzu Banda
Haile Selassie
Hassan II
Kenneth Kaunda
Jomo Kenyatta
Winnie Mandela
Mobutu Sese Seko
Robert Mugabe
Kwame Nkrumah
Julius Kambarage
    Nyerere
Anwar Sadat
Jonas Savimbi
Léopold Sédar Senghor
William V. S. Tubman

VOLUME 3: Environmental Leaders 2

John Cronin
Dai Qing
Ka Hsaw Wa
Winona LaDuke
Aldo Leopold
Bernard Martin
Cynthia Moss
John Muir
Gaylord Nelson
Douglas Tompkins
Hazel Wolf

OVER NIGHT BOOK

This book must be returned before the
first class on the following school day.

Biography Today - General Series Vol. 12 -
R Bio 920   24605

Abbey, Cheri
Pierce Middle School